MY ESCAPE

1956

MEMOIRS OF A HUNGARIAN

TEENAGE FREEDOM FIGHTER

To John and Prdride with all the best Otto Ciancelli

Reviews of the book

"This book is so exciting that it is impossible to put it down. It is like a good adventure novel except here the reader knows that all the dramatic events are true." Klára Elizabeth Schirl

"Sometimes I forgot that my job was to review and comment on the book, it is so exciting. I actually had to go back and re-read parts of it." Angie Sutera

"How wonderful that one of us saved the details of these almost forgotten memories of our challenging dangerous escape. After so many years, this little book vividly recreates the exciting events of the escape of which we all were participants. This account documents a tiny second of history for future generations". György Ürmössy, fellow escapee

"This description of our escape is a detailed eye-witness account. We are delighted that the manuscript has surfaced after 50 years. This book will remain as part of documented history." Gábor Benczúr-Ürmössy, fellow escapee

"When I read this book many years after our escape, I found it fabulous. I could not remember many of the details of our escape until I read this document. This book rejuvenated my memory and all the details of our dramatic escape are returning. Thank you for preserving them." Miklós Ürmössy, fellow escapee

"The teenage author wrote this account of our tribulations with a spirit still filled with anxiety and youthful vehemence. Every word of the story is true. This is living history." Anikó Toró-Csák, fellow escapee

MY ESCAPE

Memoirs of a Hungarian

Teenage Freedom Fighter

Written in 1956 and translated fifty years later

By

Eszter Kandó Odescalchi

Copyright 2007, 2012 by Eszter Kandó Odescalchi

All rights reserved. No part of this publication may be reproduced, distributed or transmitted without the express consent of the author.

Cover Design by Daniel N. Odescalchi
Printed and bound in the United States of America
Second edition

ISBN 0-9916-0421-0

Library of Congress Control Number: 2014904326

EOK Communications
1020 Freedom Rd
Pleasant Valley, NY 12569
Twinks.odes@gmail.com

Foreword

This book is the story of eight young refugees' dramatic escape from Hungary after Russian tanks defeated the *1956 Hungarian Revolution*. Together, they faced the dangers of the escape: Soviet tanks, secret police and border guards. Together they suffered the cold, the rain, the thick mud, the cruel reeds and the hopelessness of being lost in the swamp not knowing whether or not they would end up in the free world or face the menacing arms of Soviet guards.

In spite of all the misery, they also experienced the best manifestations of humanity: compassion, love, sacrifice and nobility.

I wrote these memoirs as a teenager in 1956, right after my arrival in Vienna and translated them from the original Hungarian document fifty years later without altering a word of my teenage diary.

To enable the reader to better understand the sequence of events and see the distances we covered during the escape, I have added pictures and maps.

Esther Kandó Odescalchi

6

The Actors in the Drama

Acknowledgements

Many thanks to my family, Edmond, Daniel, Dominic, Vida and Lee Odescalchi, Zsuzsi Kandó Berube and friends, Klári Schirl, Miklós Ürmössy, Roger Donway, and Angie and Vini Sutera for offering their editorial suggestions. A special thanks to Anikó Csák Toró for translating the book to German and to Gábor Benczúr-Ürmössy for reviewing the Hungarian and German versions.

I also want to thank my college students who suggested that I add a short historical background to the book. I am also grateful to modern technology that allows me to borrow some photos and maps from the World Wide Web's public domain.

Lecturis Salutem

Contents

Foreword 5

Dedication 10

Prologue 11

    What is Communism? 11

Epigraph 14

My Story Begins 16

    Riding the "Escapee" Train 20

    Hiding from the Russian Guards 29

    The Boys are Detained by the Guards 36

    A Stream of Bad News 39

    The Night of the Escape 43

    We Are Lost 48

    The Guards Try to Break Down the Door 52

    The Cruel Reeds 56

    Miracle! We Made It! 60

Epilogue 62

    Great Reunion -- Half a Century Later 62

    It was "Revolution" All Over Again -- an Eyewitness Account 70

    Actors in the Drama 77

    The Silent Actors 82

Historical Perspective 83

    The Bridge at Andau 83

    The Flag as a Symbol 86

The Hungarian National Anthem 87

The World Remembers the Heroes 88

Communist Mementos Belong to the Past 90

.... 91

Budapest is in Its Old Glory Again! 92

A Glance at Hungarian History 94

   Origins 94

   Mongol Invasion 94

   One Hundred Fifty Years of Turkish Occupation 95

   The 1848-1849 Hungarian Revolution 96

   World War I and the Treaty of Trianon 96

   Between the Two World Wars 97

   World War II and Yalta 98

   The Hungarian Revolution of 1956 99

   The Pan European Picnic 103

   After the Iron Curtain Crumbled 105

Under the Blessed Silhouette of the Statue of Liberty 106

   Why did the United States Not Intervene? 106

   In these United States the sky is the limit 108

   Building the Pillar 112

Dedication

I dedicate these memoirs of a Hungarian teenage "freedom fighter" to my beloved sons, Daniel and Dominic who urged me to translate the document into English.

This book covers but a short part of my life, a moment of great decision that shaped not only my life but also theirs. Had I not made that decision, they would not be who they are today. For I would have never met their beloved father, Edmond, and I would have never been able to bring into this land of liberty their wonderful grandparents, Dr. Kandó Melocco Ferenc and Maria (née Vesenyi) and their uncle Laszló.

I thank God every day for having given me such an exceptional family, such loving sons and the opportunity to live in liberty. Enjoy!

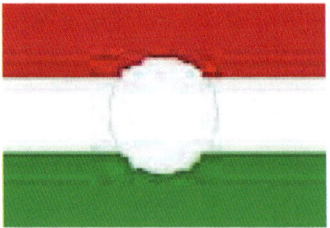

The Hungarian Flag with a hole – a symbol of the 1956 Hungarian Revolution

Prologue

What is Communism?

Communism is a cruel totalitarian regime where social order is maintained by means of terror. Freedom is an unknown concept and discrimination is carried to extremes.

Under Communism, the aristocracy, nobility, well-to-do peasantry, rich industrialists, religious leaders and intellectuals were all persecuted as "enemies of the people."

Cardinal Mindszenty at his trial in 1949

They lost their jobs, their homes, their possessions and often their lives. They were harassed, deported, or executed without trial. My Godfather, my father's brother Dr. János Melocco, was falsely accused of being a spy and hanged. He vanished one day, and the family was not allowed to inquire into his whereabouts. He left behind four small children. My father, a lawyer, lost his job at the Ministry of the Interior and supported his wife, three children and my two grandmothers by carrying heating coal on his back in huge baskets.

The pensions of both grandmothers were denied because their husbands were considered "enemies of the people."

Communism promised the proletariat everything: land, prestige, position and power. Private properties were taken away from their owners and distributed to the masses, who did not know what to do with them. For example, the soap factory where I worked in the summertime as a child was run by the facility's ex-custodian. He was functionally illiterate, screamed and yelled at us and had no clue how to run a business. No wonder the economy collapsed.

Communists carried their extreme discrimination against "enemies of the people" so far as to forbid the children of intellectuals from entering institutions of higher learning. Thus, in spite of the fact that I was the best student in my school — academically, not in behavior — I was not allowed to enter high school. I was destined to be a manual laborer for the rest of my life as were all my fellow escapees.

By 1956, the Hungarian nation had enough of the Russian Communist tyranny and the 1956 Revolution almost succeeded. However, the West was preoccupied with the Suez Canal Crisis and did not intervene militarily for fear of escalating the fighting into another world war. So the Revolution was allowed to be crushed by Soviet tanks.

The main reason my parents, and those of my escapee friends, wanted us to escape from Hungary was the discrimination against us and the total lack of opportunities for the future. *"We want you to go to the West, as much as we hate for you to leave us,"* they told me. *"Study and make a life for yourself. Under this regime, you will have no opportunities."* That is why I departed one morning, as described in this book and could not return to Hungary until years later, when in 1963 a general amnesty was given to the 1956 refugees.

Unfortunately, my parents could not escape with me because my poor grandmother was dying of cancer at the time. As soon as I became a US citizen, I sent them an invitation to immigrate to the United States. The communists, however, rejected their exit visas ten times before finally allowing them to emigrate to the United States in 1967. They were allowed to leave the country with a single suitcase in their hands.

Little Eszter whom her father Apa taught from an early age to work hard, to achieve, to face challenges with strength and dignity, not to be fussy, and most of all, to love her family, her fellow man, her country and her God.

Epigraph

Don't read these words with criticism,
Don't search for the poet in them
For it's the truth they bring to you
The story of eight desperate humans.

If you can't touch this little book
With respect, don't hold it in your hand,
For then you cannot shed a tear
For Hungary's devastated land.

With grateful love I dedicate
This book to my beloved parents
And hope that they will understand
Their loving daughter's sad lament.

Let them learn that when their child was
Left alone in the world by fate,
Far, far away in a strange land,
Her love for them always remained.

Regardless where, throughout the world,
My journey took me, all alone,
Truths my adored Mother taught me,
Like guiding posts, have always shone.

A small part of her noble soul,
From her ever-singing lips, a song:
These have led me through my journey,
And trust in God—walked me along.

Map of Hungary today

(The 1000 year old kingdom lost 2/3rd of its territory in 1920 in the Treaty of Trianon after WW I)

My Story Begins

The calendar showed November 24, 1956. My story begins here. I was 18 years old at the time. This particular Saturday started just as gray as all the other days of the losing fight for freedom. The morning was spent, as usual, searching for food, standing in line, and waiting, waiting, and waiting. Good Uncle Zimmerman (the local doctor) helped me to obtain food that day. Being a physician, he did not have to stand in line for the daily necessities (a routine during Communist days). But even he was only allowed

My beloved parents, Maria Vesenyi and Dr. Ferenc Kandó Melocco to whom I am eternally grateful.

one loaf of bread at a time. We decided to meet again later in the morning. It was then approximately 9 a.m. I rode home on my bicycle. Then I decided that I had enough time to pay a visit to Gábor Benczur-Ürmössy (my childhood friend and son of my father's buddy, Gábor Sr.) before I was to meet Dr. Zimmerman again. I wanted to find out what was happening with our planned escape from Hungary. Gábor's uncle, Géza, planned to help his two sons and some of their cousins escape from Hungary through special connections he had in a village by the Austro-Hungarian border. He promised my father he would take me along too if they went.

Having shared my plans with my Mom, I jumped on my bicycle and departed. Turning back from the gate I said, "I'll be back for lunch." On the way to Gábor's house, I met my father, Apa, who had left our home five minutes earlier. We continued bicycling together for a while. At one of the intersections I said good-bye to Apa to take a shortcut to my friend's house. Suddenly, a strange feeling came over me. "Why am I not taking the longer road with him, perhaps I won't see him for a long time." And then, as if being scared by my own thoughts, I tried bicycling faster to flee from this nightmarish idea. Fifteen minutes later, I arrived at Gábor's house. Only his grandmother was home, and she looked very distraught. She informed me that the group had just left for the train station to catch the ten o'clock express towards western Hungary. It was about quarter after ten in the morning at the time.

I will attempt the impossible, I thought. After all, in such turbulent times, the train might easily be late. Seconds later, I was pedaling toward the train station with nothing but 200 Forints (the Hungarian currency) in my pocket, which Gábor's grandmother had placed in it upon my departure. The mud from the street splattered into my face and my clothing, but I felt nothing. My bicycle sped on. I was so focused that I almost did not notice the passing military vehicles, tanks and trucks.

At one point, the road crossed a military camp where Russian soldiers were sitting in front of their tents. (Some of them thought the Danube was the Suez Canal and that they were fighting there!) They just stared blankly at nothing.

Finally, I arrived at the Kelenföld railroad station, where the crowd was as thick as fog. To find someone there, however, would have been almost impossible had it not been that Gábor was six foot six. Within a few minutes I noticed his towering figure above the mass of humanity crowding the platform.

After pushing my way through the thick crowd, I finally joined our escape group. The group's leader was uncle Géza, Gábor's uncle (and Apa's friend). He was a handsome gentleman with red cheeks and a huge mustache — a typical Hungarian-looking man.

Because he was an agricultural engineer in a village near the Austrian border, Hanságpuszta, he was able to obtain fake documents for us. According to these documents we were agricultural laborers on the farm he managed. Now the question was did he have an extra doc-

ument for me? He did—and we quickly filled it out.

The next problem was that I had absolutely no identification papers with me except for the blood-donation slip I had received at the hospital the day before. Having heard the desperate calls for blood for injured freedom fighters on the radio, I had donated blood for the first time in my life.

In spite of all odds, Uncle Géza was willing to take me along, and throughout our journey he was as good to me as a second father. Our escape group was comprised of eight people: Gábor, Uncle

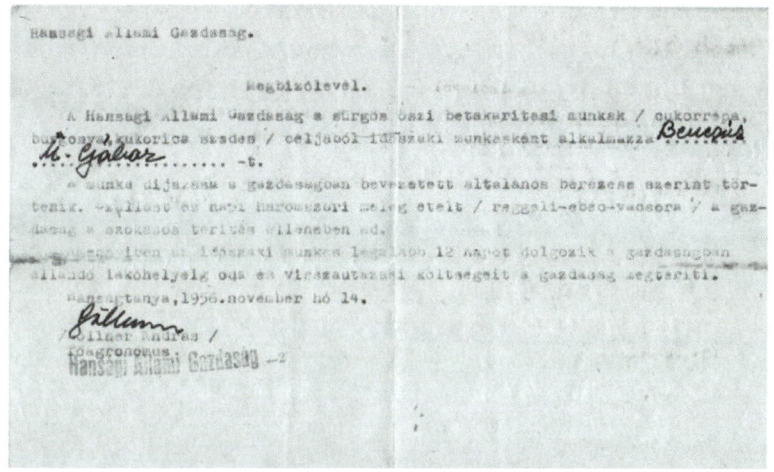

Gabor's false farm worker passport

Géza's nephew; Géza's two sons, Miklós and György; Miklós's fiancée, Sára; a young couple, András Soos ("Bandi") and his pregnant wife Mária; Anikó Csák, my classmate from grammar school and myself. Seven people in our group were ready and prepared for the dangerous journey. Only I had doubts and a terrible

internal struggle. Should I really go? Time was short. I gave my bicycle to Aunt Rosette, Gábor's mother, who had accompanied her son to the train station (she was staying behind), and I asked her to bring the news of the fake farm work permit and my departure to my father, who was chopping wood nearby at the house of a friend, Aunt Cica.

Anikó's parents and sister were also at the station, with tear-filled eyes, saying good-bye to their daughter and sister, who was about to depart into the unknown. Everyone had someone there to hug. Only I stood alone amid the crowd. But all my thoughts were with those two wonderful parents with whom God blessed me and to whom I could never be grateful enough. Whereas tears were rolling from the eyes of others, it was my soul that wept.

Riding the "Escapee" Train

Soon, the train to Győr (a city in western Hungary) rolled into the station, and the mass of humanity, like ocean waves, headed toward the cars. After a great struggle, we were also pushed on board. The train was already totally filled with would-be escapees, although nobody admitted to it. But the conductor revealed the secret by announcing: "On board to Vienna!" At that, we all looked at each other, but nobody uttered a word.

Hungary was ready for freedom

Our departing train was followed by many tear-filled eyes. It was a touching sight, indeed. At this point, I was almost happy that my sudden departure saved my parents from the burning pain of saying farewell.

The time passed quickly on board the train. Some passengers were quietly talking; some were studying maps of escape routes; yet others were munching on snacks or sleeping (if they had been lucky enough to get a seat). I was looking aimlessly out the train window, still beside myself from all the happenings around me. Never have I seen the landscape as beautiful as then. At the first station, Törökbálint, a strong voice within me started its temptation. "If you get off here," it said, "you will be home within an hour by the tram." But I stayed. No one heard my internal struggle; only God did.

In my thoughts, I said good-bye to my beloved mom about a hundred times, and turned my bicycle to the longer road, just to be with my beloved father a bit longer. Back on the train, a man approached Anikó and me and started a conversation with us. Then he handed a Viennese address to Anikó and left. We looked at each other in astonishment. How come he knew where we were heading? We had not told anyone. Who was this man? He must be a spy or an agent of ÁVÓ (Hungarian Secret Police under the Communist regime).

Were we ever relieved when, after a few more minutes, the train slowly departed from the railroad station. We never learned the identity of this strange person.

It was around 3:00 p.m. when our train arrived in Győr, our interim destination. The crowd on the platform was almost impenetrable. Somehow, however, we succeeded in getting through it and headed straight towards the bus station for Bősárkány (a village in western Hungary). There were hundreds of people there, too. One bus followed another and every one of them was attacked by a frantic crowd wanting to get on. György ran up to every vehicle to check what its destination sign said. We stood around for hours, but no bus appeared heading to "Győr-Bősárkány," our destination. Final

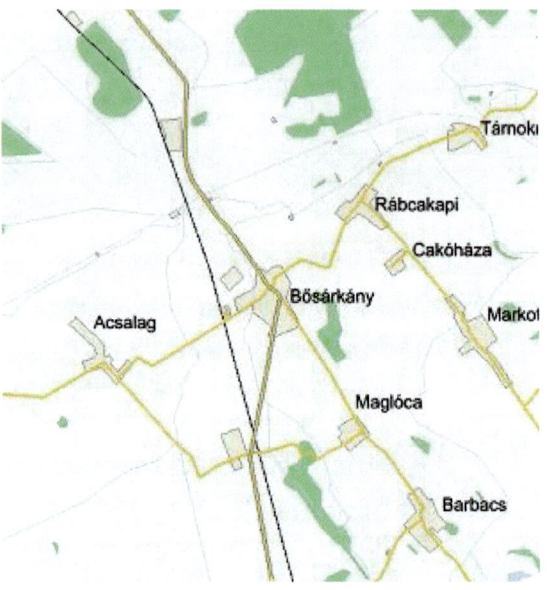

Bősárkány and vicinity

ly, we learned that our bus was not scheduled to arrive until about 6:00 p.m., a long time off. It was an ugly, damp, cloudy November afternoon. The damp cold penetrated our bones. That's when I remembered that I had left the coat that Aunt Rosette took off her back and gave me at the Budapest railroad station on the train. To pass the time, we walked up-and-down the bus station watching one bus after another — none was ours. The only advantage of the long delay was that the crowd was getting thinner and thinner around the station. Suddenly, a rather disheveled-looking female approached György, declaring that because she was alone, she would join our group of escapees whether we liked it or not. To get rid of her, we all tried our best to convince her that escape was the farthest thing from our minds. "We are farm workers," we insisted.

"Of course, of course, I understand that," she replied with a sarcastic smile, "but I will join you anyway." We spent the rest of our time at the bus station discussing how to get rid of our unwelcome intruder. Finally, the "Bősárkány" bus arrived. It was unbelievable that within a few seconds the platform was crowded once again. György, as was his custom, "attacked" this bus too, got squeezed between the bus and a tree standing next to the platform, sweeping a woman along with him. It was a challenge to drag him out of there without losing more than three of his coat buttons. Now, the struggle to get on the bus began. First, we were obliged to let residents of Bősárkány board the vehicle. The problem was that the residents almost filled the bus. After incredible pushing and pulling, we were all on board, although Gábor almost did not make it. We had to drag him into the vehicle at the last minute. When the door finally squeezed closed, it was followed by the menacing fists of the huge crowd still left standing behind. Only one person did not vent his anger, a lonely man. He stood there on the platform with tears in eyes waving farewell sadly to his departing child. It was Anikó's father.

A can of sardines would have been a roomy ballroom compared to our overcrowded bus. Yet, we were all happy to be there. The vehicle rolled along for a while on a long winding road when suddenly, the flames of a bonfire appeared ahead—the fires of the Russian guards. There will be a search, someone said. We all quietly reviewed in our minds the official lines uncle Géza made us memorize: "We are farm workers, returning from our jobs." "We are farm workers, returning from our jobs." Sure enough, the bus was stopped and we could hear an angry deep voice yelling at the driver. It was the Russian guard. He sounded like a wild animal in heat.

Thankfully, the bus driver's papers were apparently in order. The guard accepted his additional explanation that all his passengers were, indeed, local workers returning from their jobs. He motioned that the vehicle could proceed without a search.

Bősárkány

For a while nothing dramatic happened. At one point, we saw Uncle Géza make his way up to the bus driver. He handed the man 100 forints and asked him stop the vehicle among the open fields. He wanted our group to get off the vehicle before we actually reached the bus station in the village of Bősárkány. He feared that in the village proper, Russians would surely be checking our personal documents. Sure enough, after a while the bus stopped in the midst of the corn fields and we were happily filling our nearly collapsed lungs with Bősárkány's crystal-clean fresh air. At the time, evening was already on its death bed, ready to yield its dusk to the blackness of the night. Soon the fresh snow started to squeak under the boots of our little group. We were on the road toward Bősárkány, our interim destination toward Hanságpuszta.

In spite of the snow, it was an unusually dark night. Only here and there could we see some flickering lights on the horizon. And, each time, the question arose: Is it friend or foe? Everything was quiet around us. Only the footsteps of eight fleeing people indicated that there was still life left in this poor country. And even that was fading.

We had been walking barely ten minutes when suddenly the glaring lights of an automobile appeared behind us. It approached so fast that it was too late to hide. A few minutes later the vehicle stopped next to us. "Kyga uguu?" screamed a deep voice; then, without awaiting our reply, it continued: "Hy I gabau gomou"

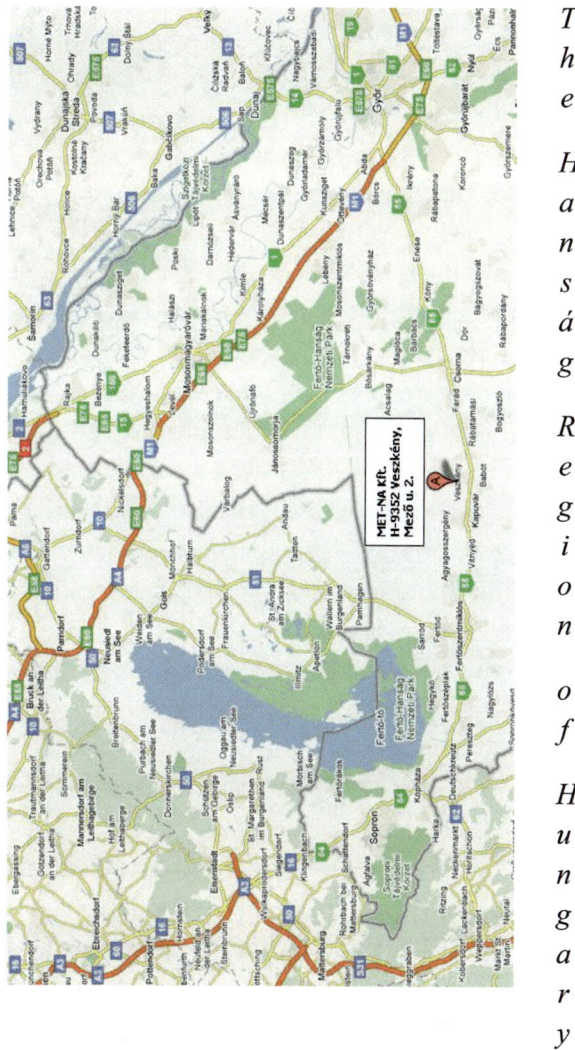

The Hanság Region of Hungary

(whatever that means in Russian). Then, to our surprise, the vehicle departed just as suddenly as it had appeared. We did not know what to do. We knew the Russians would return. Having no choice, however, we continued our journey.

A few hundred feet ahead of us, another group of refugees were walking. The vehicle stopped next to them as well, then, after few minutes, it went on its way once more. The other group also continued its journey on the frozen snowy road. Five minutes hadn't even passed when the strange car reappeared, as if growing out of the ground. All of us scattered in eight different directions, but it was too late. The huge shiny eyes of the vehicle were mercilessly glaring into our eyes. And then came the big surprise! This time, Hungarian words thundered from the lips of the three characters that had descended from the car. "You are trying to escape? You, who are so afraid of the lights of an automobile, get your act together and face the challenge!" It turned out that the three men worked in the food supply business. Therefore they were free to travel. They were merely having fun tormenting us, first with the Russian words and then with the Hungarian ones. Fortunately, Uncle Géza recognized one of the men as a fellow worker from Hanságpuszta. At that point, the man immediately turned into a nice human being and decided to help us. He warned us not to continue on the road because it would lead us straight into the arms of the Russians. "On the other side of the bridge," he explained, "a Russian tank is turning its turret towards

Search lights lit up the horizon

the road, ready for action. But you won't see it until it is too late." Having thanked the man for his warnings, we changed direction toward the Bősárkány railroad station. From there, Uncle Géza wanted to phone Hanságpuszta to find out whether the Russians were guarding the railroad bridges as well.

Within half an hour, we were huddling together at the railroad station awaiting Uncle Géza's return. The railway staff knew only too well our ultimate destination. They had given directions to hundreds of refugees who passed through the station in the past weeks. When Uncle Géza returned, he had favorable news. The railroad bridges were still safe. "Instead of following the road," he said, "we will walk along the rail tracks." And soon, our little group was stomping across the tracks almost in unison.

Tanks were everywhere

Only the high-beams of some passing cars from the faraway highway disturbed the monotony of the night's darkness.

About an hour later, we reached the first railroad bridge and crossed it without incident, stepping from railroad tie to railroad tie. A while later we reached the second rail bridge as well, which was much longer than the first one The major problem at this point was that there were houses scattered nearby and, as we crossed the bridge, jumping from one board to the next, the squeaking wood planks awakened all the dogs in the neighborhood. These otherwise sweet   animals made such an incredible commotion that we had to stop for a while and wait in the middle of the bridge. When everything quieted down, we continued our journey practically on tiptoes as much as it was possible in heavy boots. (Only I was in regular shoes.)

Finally, we reached the other side of the bridge without further problems. "One more bridge to cross," announced Uncle Géza, "and by the wee hours of the morning we should reach Bősárkány, our next destination." So we kept walking silently on the rails for two or three more hours.

Suddenly, the monotony of our walk was interrupted by an automobile from the highway that fixed its high-beams straight on our little group. To hide from the glaring flood lights, we quickly laid down on the tracks. Soon, the flood lights as bright as the noon sun surrounded us, but luck was on our side. Once again, we quickly threw ourselves on the tracks and waited motionless until the car was gone.

Finally, we reached the third rail bridge and succeeded in crossing it without incident. We had arrived in Hanságpuszta and were heading toward a cow barn on the outskirts of the village for shelter. Uncle Géza suggested that we approach the barn by traversing the open fields rather than walking on the streets. "It would be too dangerous to go into the village proper," he cautioned. Taking his advice, we ran down the railroad embankment and ran straight into a barbed-wire fence.

Fortunately, none of us was seriously injured. Our garments suffered a few ripped holes, but we were relatively unscathed. Even for me, only my gloves became victims of this adventure, having gotten tangled in the wire.

It took a while to free each other from the sharp teeth of the fence. We continued our journey through the field. Soon, however, we found ourselves in the midst of a thistle field. The dried-up, thorny bushes clung to our clothing like glue. Within half an hour, some of us seemed to be carrying a heap of prickly hay stacks on our backs. Some of the hay slowly made its way into our necks, and like a thousand needles, kept pricking every inch of exposed skins.

Hiding from the Russian Guards

As we approached a lonely ranch, all the dogs of the neighborhood awakened and ran towards us, growling and baring their sharp teeth. It was not an easy walk. From the rear, thistle bushes were one barrier, and from the front, menacing barking dogs were about to attack us. Finally, the designated barn was in sight. We stopped and waited until Uncle Géza went ahead to make sure the coast was clear.. Fortunately, everything seemed OK and soon we were enjoying the cozy animal warmth that radiated from the gentle cows that lived in the barn.

In one corner of the stable, fresh hay was spread on the floor for our comfort. The stable master, Karcsi, whose room opened onto the stable, allowed us to make some hot tea on his wood stove. He was a very nice fellow. Soon, sitting on the straw, we were sipping hot tea and eating a few bites of bread. Watching the

How they squeaked!

wonderful innocent eyes of a little calf nearby was a beautiful relief in midst of those challenging times. Having successfully reached one of our milestones by reaching the stable, Uncle Géza became very upbeat. "If we succeeded this far," he commented happily, "the rest is nothing." Having thus reassured us, he departed to fetch our local guide, who had promised to lead us across the Hungarian-Austrian border to liberty. In the meantime, one by one, we ended up in Karcsi's room, where we could listen to the broadcasts of Radio Free Europe. Several village people were also in the room, and they informed us that as of today, it was no longer as easy to cross the border as it had been only three days ago. Although the news did not sound encouraging, we trusted Uncle Géza. When the radio started to talk about refugee-related news, it was bad. The announcer said that strong re-enforcements had arrived in the very area where we were, and heavy clashes occurred between border guards and local miners. Now, more than ever, all our hopes lay in Uncle Géza.

When he finally returned, the very way he walked into Karcsi's room revealed that he had bad news too. "No guides are available anymore," he announced. "Nobody wants to risk his life for a few hundred Forints. We must spend the night here. Let's hope tomorrow will bring better luck".

Some members of our group nervously paced the stable floor; others laid down on the straw, while Uncle Géza and I continued to listen to Radio Free Europe. Later that evening, Uncle Géza, György, and I went to

Uncle Géza's local work-related lodging (a room in a peasant house) and brought back some of his blankets for our group. While we walked the muddy village streets, we kept hearing gun blasting from the direction of the Austro-Hungarian border. It was an upsetting and frightening sound.

Arriving back at the stable, we spread the blankets over the sleeping members of our group. I went back to Karcsi's room to listen to the radio. The real temptation, however, was the warm fire burning in his stove. It was wonderful to warm up again. I stayed there until around 1 a.m. when the rest of the villagers started to go home.

When I went back to the stable, everything was quiet. Only György was pacing up and down amongst the cows in an attempt to calm his nerves. I lay down on the straw next to Anikó and a bit later György joined us too. We spent the night pulling the shared blanket off of each other. The cement floor was terribly cold with only a few wisps of straw scattered on it. It felt as if we were lying on ice. I could hardly wait for daybreak.

Gábor's long body was stretched across our heads diagonally, and when he got bored of lying down, he started exercising against the one-meter-high walls that divided the stalls.

Toward daybreak, the animals started to awaken, and so did our group—those of them who had slept, that is. Karcsi brought in a small basin of water so we could wash our hands. What a treat it was and how we needed it. After all, we had been travelling for almost 48 hours without an opportunity to wash up. I amused myself watching the adorable little calves suckle their moms. I can do that too, I thought, and submerged my fingers into the warm milk pail and let the little calves gently suckle the milk off of them.

Around 6:30 a.m., Anikó and I decided to look around a bit in the vicinity of the stable. We did not find anything exciting but on our way back, two young men suddenly joined us. They were escapees too, but the Russians had already caught them twice — they were lucky that the Hungarian guards let them go. Having spent the night in an open-air shed, the young men were desperate for a warmer place. We let them follow us back to the stable.

When we arrived there, our group was ready to head to its next destination, the house of the Gombkötő family, who lived nearby. Once again, we found it wise to traverse the open field instead of the streets. The Gombkötős were kind enough to offer us one of their rooms.

Meanwhile, one of the young men who had joined us earlier went to fetch the rest of his group. While he was gone, Anikó and I were angrily reprimanded for bringing yet others to join us, when we ourselves were there at the mercy of our hosts.

Beehive oven

Within half an hour, we arrived at the Gombkötős and enjoyed the real Hungarian hospitality of the family. This wonderful peasant family had seven children, arranged like pipe organs, from two-year-old Jancsi all the way to sixteen-year-old Erzsike. I could never have imagined that children could be so well behaved, independent and disciplined as these were. Little Jancsi could eat alone with a fork and knife. Four-year-old little Évi shined her shoes alone, not an easy task considering the thick mud of the Hanság (the swampy area around Hanság lake).

One could not have expected better behavior from a group of grown-ups. And to think that all seven children shared one medium–sized peasant room! Furthermore, as unbelievable as it sounds, and in spite of seven children, there wasn't a wrinkle on the high-bed. (In peasant homes, many pillows and blankets are placed upon each other, so the made-up bed often reaches the ceiling.) Nor was there a speck of dirt on the floor. There was such order everywhere; it was as if a group of angels lived there instead of seven youngsters.

The Gombkötős were wonderful people. Hardly ten minutes after our arrival, our frozen stiff, exhausted bodies enjoyed the warmth of the flickering fireplace, and we could watch the impish play of the flaming dried corn cobs used for the fire. The warmth of the fire and the wonderful family atmosphere immediately awakened our appetites. Within a half an hour we were happily sharing a great Hungarian breakfast on a tulip-decorated table cloth: bacon on soft, fresh, homemade bread. The hot tea our hostess served us warmed our bodies from inside, and the crackling fire from the outside. This dual comfort, combined with our hosts' warm

Warm Hungarian bread

Muddy boots

hospitality, totally renewed the spirit of our pitifully exhausted group. After breakfast, we gathered around the fireplace on blankets spread around the floor. Anikó, Gábor, György, and I even shared a card game.

Meanwhile, there were serious discussions going on about the future of our group, how should we proceed, where could we find a guide, what should we do next? Soon it was almost noontime. Thanks to Uncle Géza's local position (he worked in the district as agricultural engineer), he was entitled to use the local workers' kitchen. Luckily, he succeeded in arranging to get some food for us too. The food was truly excellent and the portions were large enough for an elephant.

After helping clean the dishes, we spent the rest of the afternoon talking and playing cards. In the meantime, one visitor after another came to the house, bringing news about the current state of affairs that would influence the progress of our escape. Unfortunately, the news was all negative. Poor Uncle Géza was forever scouting around the village to ensure that we missed no opportunity for escape.

This was the fate of many

After dark, our entire group headed down to the workers' dining room for some food. However, the walk wasn't as easy as it sounds. On the unpaved streets of the village, the liquefied mud of the Hanság region poured into our shoes with each step we took. The female members of the group wearing light shoes had it especially difficult.

The workers' dining room was an elongated hall with long tables and benches constructed of rough, splintery wood. It was a dark and dreary place.

The only source of light came from small kerosene lamps that flickered on every table. The hall was full of would-be escapees. It was easy to distinguish these from the local villagers by their "city" clothes and their exhausted, sleep-deprived, bleary eyes. After dinner, Uncle Géza introduced us one by one to the director of the Communist-run communal farm where he worked. We did not see too much of each other however, because the dining room was very dark. Later on, this became the source of quite a calamity. After finishing our meal, the women returned to the Gombkötő family for the night. The male members of our group joined Uncle Géza in his local residence, a small unheated room in the village. The women remained in the family's home where two beautiful white "high-beds" awaited us. I shared one with Anikó, whereas Maria slept in the other. Sára took the day bed in the corner of the room.

Soon everything was quiet but I could not fall asleep. Strange thoughts were swirling around in my head. I saw the Austro-Hungarian border; I saw guards jumping out from every bush; I saw myself among the imprisoned escapees. I was in an open truck speeding toward a Siberian labor camp or ready to be executed. But nothing was as bad as the feeling that came over me when my thoughts went home to my beloved parents. I felt so guilty. Is this what they deserved from me? How could I abandon them like this? What hurt me most was the thought that perhaps my dear parents imagined me lying somewhere in a dark frozen ditch and that that horrible thought would not let them sleep either. And there I was, safe and sound in a nice clean warm bed with no way of letting them know I was OK. Such thoughts tormented me for hours, until merciful sleep finally let me escape into a wonderful worry-free world of peace.

The Boys are Detained by the Guards

Early the next morning, Uncle Géza and the boys arrived back at the Gombkötős. Once again, our breakfast was good Hungarian bread, paprika bacon, and tea. After breakfast, the "boys" — Bandi, Miklós, Gábor, and György — went to work on Uncle Géza's communal farm. After having cleaned up the room, we girls worked on the lovely tapestry Aunt Erzsi was working on. Around 2:30 p.m., the boys returned to the house very excited. "Imagine," they yelled, "in the pouring rain, on the way to the dried-up corn field, a Russian guard pulled us off the truck. He obviously saw from our clothing that we did not belong with the village folks. We tried to explain to him every which way that we were workers, but he would not listen and was determined to lock us up. It was only after the vehement protests of the local peasants that the guards finally let us go." During this time, Communist agricultural practices made no sense. Everything was dictated from the central government. The government arbitrarily decided on a date to plow, to plant and to harvest. People were forced to work on the fields, rain or shine, and harvest fruits even when they were not yet ripe; in general their decisions made no sense to knowledgeable farmers.

No spot was safe

This incident made us very upset. On top of it, only bad news came from the visiting local peasants. The situation was getting worse by the minute. It was becoming more and more difficult to escape.

We spent the afternoon planning and playing cards. Meanwhile, Bandi got very ill. He developed a high fever and chills from being out on the field all day in the pouring rain — it was November in Hungary, after all.

The rain did not let up all day. In the evening, we decided to bring home dinner instead of going to the communal dining room. I went with Uncle Géza and György to pick up the food. By then, the mud was almost up to our knees and it took us forever to reach the soup kitchen, a mere kilometer (.62 miles) away. We brought back wonderful cold pork in aspic (kocsonya) and fresh Hungarian bread.

After dinner, I went with Aunt Erzsi and one of her daughters to Karcsi's house to listen to Radio Free Europe. Unfortunately, we heard nothing encouraging. However, when the usual report on refugees came on, the radio announced that in spite of all the new challenges, another 2000 people had succeeded crossing the Austro-Hungarian border. Uncle Géza lamented, "How I wish there were 2008!" That evening, sleeping arrangements were the same as the night before. Once again, I could hardly close my eyes. The uncertainty, and the idleness, got on my nerves.

The following day started off the same as the day before. We girls stayed behind and continued work on Aunt Erzsi's needlepoint, whereas the boys went off to work on the farm. At noon, we all walked down to the communal kitchen to have lunch with the boys.

We had hardly started on the delicious gulyás soup when the boys entered the hall in great excitement. The same thing had happened as the day before, only this time it was worse. This time a different Russian guard yanked them off the carriage and would not let them go. He did not believe the villagers' claims about their being regular workers and escorted all of them into the farm director's office for identification. The director, to whom we had been introduced two nights before in the dark hall of the dining room, did not recall meeting the boys and told the Russian so. It was only after György reminded him that he was Uncle Géza's son did the director recant his story and confirmed that the boys were in fact his "new" workers. At that, the Russian guard had to leave without further ado. Nothing earth-shaking happened that afternoon. When evening came, however, it was no longer advisable to venture out to the dining room. So our wonderful hosts, the Gombkötős, provided us with dinner.

The rain, sleet and snow did not let up all day and all night. Bandi, who was quite ill by then, decided not to go to Uncle Géza's unheated room but stay with us girls instead. His wife was only too happy to share her bed with him.

After dark, once again I went to Karcsi's place to listen to Radio Free Europe. I was desperate for any updates. The news was dire. The radio announced that fresh troops had arrived in Hungary's Hanság region, where we were, and that night hardly any refugees had succeeded in crossing the border to Austria.

A Stream of Bad News

The train was blown up by the communists

Upon my return from Karcsi's room to the Gombkötős there was plenty to talk about. But we had to whisper all evening because by then Bandi was very ill and we did not want to disturb him. Early the next morning, Bandi had to mimic sleep, turning toward the wall, so that we girls could wash up. Later, after the boys arrived from Uncle Géza's room, we sat down to the breakfast table once again. Suddenly, Aunt Erzsi burst into the room all excited. She had just heard that during the night, five dead bodies had been carried into the village from the border. They had been shot dead by the guards. "And," she continued, "new re-enforcements arrived at the border with the order to shoot. No refugee succeeded in crossing the border last night," she added in tears. "The order is to shoot."

It now became evident that the longer we waited the worse the situation would get. We all realized that we must act and act now. As a precaution, the boys did not go to work that day. Why expose them again? The only sign of life all morning was the coming and goings of the boys carrying in the dried corn cobs to feed our fire.

Meanwhile, poor Uncle Géza trudged through the muddy streets of the village, trying to find a guide for our group. The helpless idleness started to get on everybody's nerves. Anikó and I decided that the next day we would attempt to escape on our own even if nobody from the group joined us. To make matters worse, Maria was perpetually crying thinking about her widowed mother, whom she had left behind. These were difficult hours.

The next day was already Thursday. Uncle Géza left the house early again to search for a guide and when he returned, he happily announced that we were departing at 3:00 p.m. that afternoon. The plan was to obtain some workers' clothes for all of us, and dressed like peasants, we would get on a carriage toward the border. The hope was that the guards would think that we were workers returning home from the field. That way, we were hoping to reach the village of Hanságfalva, three kilometers away without arousing suspicion. From Hanságfalva, under the cover of night, we would attempt to sneak across the border somehow. A few hours later, angelic Aunt Erzsi came into the room asking us whether we would like to write a few words to our relatives. A villager was heading to Budapest on the midday train. He offered to take our notes. Within seconds, eight eager pens were busily writing to their loved ones. We placed the eight little slips of paper into an envelope and off they went – so we hoped.

Less than an hour passed when Aunt Erzsi re-entered the room in great excitement: "The train to Budapest was attacked and blown up. The Russians gathered all the passengers with Budapest addresses and took them away. The local people were told to walk home. My poor sweethearts," she continued sobbing, "you don't have too much hope. You cannot escape anymore, yet they won't let you go home either." "The more reason we must try to escape," yelled one of the boys, breaking the deadly silence. The arm of the clock moved slowly, as if it too was walking in the Hanság mud. Finally, Uncle Géza arrived with the work clothes — a bunch of worn, torn, rather dirty garments, but what difference did it make at that point? Around 2:30 p.m., we started to get dressed and soon, our group of beggars stood by the door nervously waiting for the carriage to arrive. Our entire appearance reflected the sad state of the working class under Communism (a social class that was promised heaven on earth). A few minutes later, Aunt Erzsi returned to the room accompanied by a strange woman, also an escapee. She wanted to follow her husband to the free world and was determined to join us. Fortunately, there was a garment for her too. The boys looked particularly awful. They wore funny looking hats that had seen better days. The rain had soaked them totally out of shape. Instead of being straight above their eyes, the brims hung down into their eyes, obscuring their faces and their vision. They looked adequately terrible. We waited for the magic hour of three o'clock with great anticipation. But three o'clock came and went, and our vehicle was nowhere to be seen. Uncle Géza departed again to find out what had happened. Within a half an hour

The ugly dirty hat

he returned very discouraged. "You can remove your outfits now" he said sadly, "we won't need them anymore. The coach man has changed his mind and does not dare to take the risk. I can't blame him," he added. "The events of the past 24 hours are good enough reason for his decision. We must make the trip on foot under the cover of the night. We must wait until it gets dark." We had hardly removed our dirty oil-laden uniforms when Aunt Erzsi entered the room with a big smile: "I found another driver," she announced happily. "He will be here within half an hour." Having had practice in donning working cloths, within five minutes we were dressed again. Once again, we waited and waited, looking out the kitchen window, watching the road which was hardly visible through the rain that obscured our vision like a thin spider-web. As we stood there, the minutes ticked by, and still no coach was in sight. About an hour later, very disappointing news came once again. The second driver had chickened out too. "We must proceed on foot," announced Uncle Géza. "I am so sorry for those of you who don't have proper shoes. But," he added, "at this point we have no choice." Once again, like puppets moved by strings, we took off our workers' overalls, and within minutes we were ready to go. Meanwhile, Uncle Géza spread out a local area map that our host had provided and started to review the possible escape routes. He admitted having visited this area only once. It was during the day by car, and he had not paid particular attention to the road.

The search lights pierced through the forest

However, our hosts gave us some useful hints for our adventure. "Follow the embankment all the way until you reach the uncut corn fields," they told us. "When you notice the huge mountains of hay in the distance, make a detour because the Russian guards usually hide behind them. Once you reach the brook at the edge of the woods, proceed with extra care and by all means avoid the bridge at Hanságfalva, because that is a favorite hiding place of the guards."

The Night of the Escape

Uncle Géza asked all of us to remove everything from our bags except for the most essential items to make them lighter for the challenge ahead. I did not have to worry. I had nothing in my possession but an empty wallet. The sad moment of saying farewell to the Gombkötős had arrived. Aunt Erzsi sobbed with as much emotion as if she were saying goodbye to her own children.

After having hugged each one of us, my hosts motioned that I should follow them into the other room. "Honey, don't go," they begged me. "Stay with us. Where there is room for seven, there is room for eight." Their love and affection deeply touched me. "Thank you so very much," I responded, tears welling up threatening to spill over. Hugging both of my hosts, I said, "You are the best and I love you, but I must to go. Thank you. Thank you for everything."

Soon, our little group was on its way. Quietly, like bandits in action, we were making our way out of the small village that had protected us for the past few days. It was dark. Only a few faint lights flickered far away through the mist and incessantly pouring rain.

Search lights and flares lit up the rainy sky

Within minutes, our feet were totally soaked. There were large pot holes, filled with water everywhere on the road, and we kept stumbling into them in the inky darkness.

We lined up in pairs. Our leader was Uncle Géza, followed by Bandi, then Miklós with Sára, then György and I, finally, Gábor with Anikó on his arm. The strange lady who had joined our group was also among us. According to plan, we walked quietly without uttering a word.

It took us about ten minutes to reach the end of the friendly proximity of the village houses. Beyond the village, the road was getting worse by the minute. At one point, Uncle Géza stopped and gathered us around him for a quick briefing. "It would be wise to leave the road and proceed on the grassy plains" he suggested. "You would be less likely noticed there."

He was right. We had hardly started to walk again when suddenly searchlights flared up in the sky. It was like the grand finale of a fireworks show. Judging by their illuminating power, the flares originated from nearby, exposing our desperate group of escapees. We quickly fell to the wet ground for cover.

When the illumination died down, we started to walk again, but within minutes the searchlights shot up from the opposite direction, forcing us to the ground again. By then, we were wet and muddy from head to toe and shivering in the cold. We stopped and deliberated. All of us knew that reality did not seem to favor us, and we all agreed that our chance of success was only about one percent. Reassured with such positive prospects, we continued our journey into the unknown.

From then on, we had to throw ourselves onto the ground every five minutes to avoid being noticed by the merciless searchlights all around us. After a seemingly endless walk, we finally reached the hay mound our hosts had warned us about. In front of us was a ditch about one meter (three feet) deep that snaked along between the road and the hay.

Because the road was too dangerous at this point, we continued through the corn field among the still-standing corn stalks. Suddenly, we heard faint noises approaching. We quickly dropped to the ground and nervously waited. Soon, the faint noises turned into approaching footsteps and the loudly thumping frightened heartbeats of our desperate group echoed from the mud below. The footsteps drew nearer and nearer and finally they passed us by about fifteen feet away. Then they slowly disappeared in the nearby woods. It was a close call, but they could have been other refugees.

With a collective inner sigh of relief, we continued our perpetual struggle with the thick mud of the Hanság region. Nothing unusual happened for a while, other than the flares being shot up every five minutes, when we heard footsteps from the direction of the hay mound. Once again, we were forced to lay still face down in the mud.

Dangerous lights were flickering from afar

Suddenly, an entire army of flares was shot into the air, creating daylight conditions. The light exposed a group of people heading straight in our direction. Obviously, they were refugees too. While on the ground, we waited until the group passed us by. We did not join them because a large group would have been easier to spot.

We continued once again, although the mud of the corn field made our advance almost impossible. It became so bad that we decided to continue our journey on the road after all. From far away, we could hear the humming of a tank's motor. It sounded like a gigantic mosquito buzzing about. On the horizon we could also see the flickering lights of some heavy-duty vehicles.

György and I suddenly noticed a yellow beam creating a gigantic semicircle in the distance. It was slowly approaching

The corn stalks hid us

the road. When the beam seemed to reach the road, it stopped. At this point the light got so small, and seemed so far away, that we did not pay particular attention to it. Suddenly, however, the innocent little light turned into a strong floodlight that lit up the entire area, totally exposing all of us.

We quickly moved into the bushes surrounding the roadside. From the sudden motion, poor Sára slipped into the knee-deep water of the nearby ditch submerging half of her body. To pull her out of her unintended frozen bath, poor Géza bacsi and Miklós had to wade into the frozen muddy water too.

After having removed Sára from the muddy ditch, we decided to leave the road again and proceed diagonally away from it through an endless corn field. On this badly planned, communist-run, centrally maintained, communal farm, the corn stalks were still uncut and their dried leaves whispered in the November rain like thousands of gossiping old ladies. Meanwhile, the illumination lasted several more torturous minutes.

Because of the terrible noise created by our bodies moving through the corn stalks, we decided to slow our pace. We struggled through this infinite field for several more hours. I can still hear the monotonous sad whispers of the frozen dead plants. They did provide us with one advantage. They were good cover against the endless flares being shot up around us.

In the dark they looked so frightening

When the corn field finally ended, we found ourselves dangerously near the aforementioned haystacks. Carefully and quietly, we slowly tiptoed away from the dangerous mounds. Meantime, the rain, which had slacked off a bit in the past few hours, started once again with full vengeance. The ground was becoming completely soaked and we kept stumbling across huge water-filled holes. We could see the flickering lights of the guards all around us.

We Are Lost

It was around 1:00 a.m. when Uncle Géza suddenly stopped and confessed that he had no idea where we were. "We are totally lost," he announced. This dismal announcement made us all terribly worried, for he was our trusted, guiding light. After a short discussion, we continued our struggle with the mud relying now only on our instincts. None of us had any idea what direction to take. Yet, we walked on.

About an hour later, we arrived at the edge of a dark forest. This was another of our landmarks toward the border as our guide explained before he left us. This landmark reassured us that we were proceeding in a westerly direction. Our discouraged hearts were filled with renewed energy to go on. We could also hear the gushing water of the brook that ran at the front of the forest. It was another of our landmarks. Suddenly, like thunder, loud male voices hit our ears. The blood froze in our veins. We knew that refugees were quiet. Therefore the voices must be coming either from the secret police or Russian soldiers. The voices were getting nearer and nearer and soon we could hear a bunch of heavy footsteps approaching. Throwing ourselves to the ground, flattening our bodies into the mud, we waited.

Just then, György had an uncontrollable attack of coughing. Because of our critical situation the poor guy had to bury his face into his hat, nearly choking himself to death. Meanwhile, the footsteps were coming straight towards us. I already felt the yoke of Communist hands upon my shoulder. The group came so near to our prostrated bodies that the heavy boots almost stepped on us. They were guards, indeed. Yet, apparently they missed us and passed us by. To this day, I don't understand how we were not caught.

The danger now gone, we continued our journey towards the direction of the brook. At one point, we stopped under a huge tree by the water's edge while Uncle Géza crossed over to the other side of the stream to investigate the terrain. We could hear the crackling of the dried branches under his heavy boots, signaling that he had reached the forest.

Because his huge boots made so much noise, we were convinced that the nearby guards would notice him. Soon, however, he returned with the good news that all was OK and suggested that we cross over to the other side. Wading into the knee-deep icy water, he helped us one by one to the other side. Because the stream was quite wide, we all got our share of drenching. In addition, our slipping and sliding created so much commotion and noise that it could have easily cost us our liberty, perhaps even our lives. Finally, we all made it to the other side, hiding in the forest. Broken dried-up branches littered the ground among the trees, making our journey not only difficult but also dangerous. We could move only at a snail's pace because the squeaking, crackling underbrush created so much noise. But by then we were ready for the worst. When we successfully reached a sort of road, none of us knew what direction to take. After a short conference, we gambled on a direction and proceeded into the unknown. After walking for about half an hour, scattered lights became visible from among the tree trunks through the nearby forest. Were these stationary or moving lights? Moving objects, such as we ourselves were, often have the impression that the lights they see are in motion as well, even if they are not. We stopped to determine what the lights were all about. It did not do any good, however. Even from a standing position we could not conclude whether the lights were moving or not. Our group became totally divided on the subject. Some members swore they saw them move, whereas other felt they stood still.

Next to us lay another huge field covered with still standing dry corn stalks. Like a group of goslings we started to walk through them one after another in a straight line. Then we noticed the flickering lights ahead of us on the horizon again.

We stopped once more to assess the situation. Once again we could not come to a consensus, so we continued. Soon it became clear that the lights we saw through the trees were coming from the windows of Hanságpuszta's stables, our next destination. The prospect of the security of the stables rejuvenated us. We almost forgot our frozen feet, our wet clothes, and our grumbling empty stomachs. In a little while, we arrived at a huge barn and Uncle Géza unlocked the gigantic stable door. The clicking of the large lock indicated that we had reached safety and a temporary resting place. Having entered the building, Uncle Géza firmly locked the gargantuan wooden door behind us. The monotonous even breathing of the cattle comforted our tormented souls and relaxed our tired bodies. We were ready to join the animals in a land of anguish-free dreams. There was a pile of fresh straw in the stable's corner that provided excellent sleeping quarters for our exhausted limbs. Our first deed was to remove our soaked shoes and try to warm our frozen toes. Meanwhile, the rain finally stopped hammering the red tiled roofs of the tiny hamlet. From amongst the broken clouds, the moon seemed to be trying to peek at the tragic sadness of the Hungarian countryside. Later, he got so bold as to peek through the cracks of the stable door, illuminating our refugee group. To avoid being noticed by raiding guards, we stuffed hay into the door cracks.

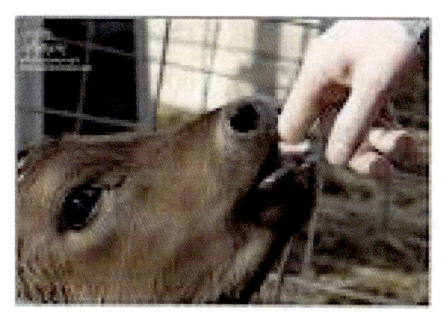

The warm comfort of the stable soon loosened our heretofore sealed lips, until Uncle Géza warned us. "Please don't think we are safe here. For the past few nights, Russians and the secret police have been sweeping through area stables looking for refugees." That news quickly quieted us down. Slowly, we all found our little places on the straw and cuddled up to whoever was near to us for warmth. Our coats became our blankets. Our departure time was fixed for 3:00 a.m. One of Uncle Géza's local friends offered to lead us through the most critical part — towards the border crossing but not all the way to Austria.

Again, I could not sleep a wink. My entire body was shaking from the cold. My worst problem was that I could no longer feel my wet icy feet. My toes were painfully numb. For a long time I talked to Uncle Géza, who was sitting on the straw next to me. On my other side was György. We placed György's coat under us; my jacket and Uncle Géza's coat served as blanket for the three of us. Soon everybody was asleep, only Uncle Géza and I kept up our vigil. After a while, Uncle Géza complained that he was terribly hungry and had nothing to eat. We knew that the only person who had some food in his bag was Bandi. However, his bag was somewhere on the other side of the stable on the straw. I offered to find the precious bundle. So I crept slowly between my sleeping friends toward Bandi's food bag but accidentally fell over poor sleeping Bandi, who wasn't particularly pleased with this method of awakening. After many excuses and a feeble protest, he gave me his bag of food anyway.

The Guards Try to Break Down the Door

Having satisfied his tormenting hunger, Uncle Géza finally fell asleep too. I was in charge of watching the clock for our 3:00 am meeting with our guide. Staying awake wasn't a challenge for me, because somehow I wasn't sleepy at all.

A village house

It was probably around 1:00 a.m. that heavy fists started banging on the huge stable door. Inside, everybody suddenly awakened. The unexpected alarm paralyzed us and made us afraid even to breathe. . "Immediately open the door!" thundered a crude male voice from the outside. Uncle Géza motioned that we should not move. "Open up, or we break down the door," continued several loud voices in unison. We still did not move. Then the banging intensified and continued incessantly. Still, there was no response from us. Only the rattling of the chains of the suddenly awakened cows responded to the threats.

As a result of all the banging, the dry straw we had stuck into the door cracks fell out, and the lights of the oil lamps the intruders held in their hands seemed to illuminate the entire stable. The banging, the menacing, and the yelling continued for at least fifteen endless minutes. "We know you are there. Come out now on your own. You'll be better off. If we have to come in and get you, you'll all be dead." We still did not move. Finally, the invading group gave up and left into the dark night as quietly as it had appeared.

Afterwards, Uncle Géza explained to us that many refugee groups, exhausted and nervous, get so scared from the banging and threatening that they open up the door and get immediately arrested and taken away. Around 2:30 am, we started getting ready for the final stretch of our escape. Uncle Géza was desperately trying to find his socks that he had placed on the back of a sleeping cow to dry. What he did not expect was that the cow would turn over during the night and bury his precious clothing underneath her warm body. We tried and tried again to coax the huge herbivore to get up, but she would not budge. So poor Uncle Géza had to put his bare feet into his cold wet boots. His socks remained buried under the sleeping animal.

Soon, we were on the village street again, proceeding carefully to avoid being detected. Upon reaching the protective shade of an empty house, we stopped and waited for a while. Uncle Géza departed to find our guide. We squeezed our bodies to the wall as flat as was humanly possible. No sooner did Uncle Géza leave than a male figure appeared and headed straight in the direction of our group. From his causal behavior, however, it soon became evident that he did not yet notice us. Not knowing whether he was friend or foe at such an early hour of the morning, we squeezed even further to the side of the house. A giant weeping willow stood about fifteen yards away from us on the roadside. Suddenly, changing direction, the stranger headed directly to the tree. And there, he did something that dogs do, not exactly for ladies to see. We were all holding our breaths in profound silence, but one of the boys in our group found this sight so amusing that he let out an audible giggle.

At that, the stranger looked up and headed straight toward us. It turned out that he was a stable hand heading to work and on the way, nature called. The poor guy was most embarrassed, but we were most relieved.

Uncle Géza finally returned with our guide who promised to lead us for a while but not all the way to the Austrian border. He did not want to take the risk. Before starting on our way, he gave us all sorts of tips and instructions for the next leg of our dangerous journey. "There are two guard stations near each other by the bridge which we must cross," he explained. "Therefore, we must proceed with utmost caution. Be prepared to stop often during our trip" he continued, "just to look, listen and assess the situation." The stable hand, who still stood nearby, also gave us some useful hints. Being a native of the area, he was familiar with the border region.

Soon, we were on our way towards our final destination: Austria and liberty. Leaving the village, we slowly and carefully walked in the forest that encircled Hanságfalva heading toward the bridge. Every so often we stopped, listened, and assessed our safety.

In about half an hour we reached the little bridge. The nearby Russian guard building was totally illuminated, including the giant red star on top of it. Huge flood lights were set up in front of it, fixing their menacing and merciless eyes on the little bridge, ready to snag those who dared to cross it. "No one seems to be here right now;" said our guide, "let's go."

As we crawled onto the bridge, its wooden planks squeaked and creaked mercilessly. We had to slow down, and with utmost caution, climb on all fours one after another.

I am convinced that the only reason the Russians did not catch us was that they probably did not expect anyone in his right mind to attempt to cross such an illuminated bridge right next to their headquarters. And fortunately, the Russian border patrol wasn't paying enough attention to the bridge at that particular time.

We finally succeeded in reaching the other side of the bridge. But we soon realized that we had landed on a road leading straight to the main gate of the guards' headquarters building. The flood light around the building created nearly day-light conditions. Hunched over like animals, crawling on the ground, we tried to get away from that dangerous spot.

Once we were far enough from the guard building, one of the most touching moments of our escape occurred. Uncle Géza bade farewell to his children. He had to remain in Hungary because of other family obligations. He and our guide did not dare to accompany us any further. They both had to return to the village.

This was a moving moment for all of us. He hugged each of us with a loving paternal embrace and wished us well. Indeed, in a sense we were all his children! Before departing, our guide gave us a set of instructions on how to proceed. "Now, we are about one kilometer from the Austrian border" he explained. "If you take this path, it will lead you straight into Austria. No forks or detours. This path ends at the border ditch separating Austria from Hungary. If you reach that," he continued, "you must cross a small bridge again and you will be on Austrian soil.

"In Austria, the International Red Cross will pick you up on the highway. The organization is scouting the area day and night for refugees." With that, he and Uncle Géza turned around to go back to a sad land of slavery and turmoil. Now, we were on our own and like freshly hatched goslings, we proceeded in a straight line, one after another.

Our new leader was Miklós, Uncle Géza's older son, about 23 at the time. (We respected him, because of his age – already 23!) He stopped us about every hundred feet to assess the situation. We followed his every move and obeyed all his instructions just as freshly hatched goslings would respond to their mother.

The Cruel Reeds

The path was getting muddier and muddier until it completely swallowed our shoes. Soon the supposed path started to disappear altogether and the endless watery mess got deeper and deeper with every step. At times, the reeds grew into the middle of our little pathway, at other times the path led through chopped-down vegetation. Soon we noticed a few trees far away. To us, every one of them looked like Russian guards ready to shoot us. As we kept walking, I was silently praying to the Holy Mother: "Help me now, oh merciful Virgin Mother. You have the power to disperse sorrow and grief. Where the power of man stops, yours does not end. Help me now, oh merciful Mary, Amen." I must have said my silent prayer at least a hundred times, but the border was still nowhere in sight. At the next stop it became clear that none of us had any idea where we were and in what direction we were heading. The one thing all of us agreed upon was that we had already walked at least twice the distance of what our local guide had indicated. So we continued our journey into the unknown. Suddenly, the little ingrown path came to a fork. It confused us even more. Our guide said nothing about a fork. Where were we? Which way was west? Finally, following sheer instinct, we took the path to the left. A few yards away on the right side of the path we noticed a ditch full of water. We stopped again. Could this be the border moat? How wonderful that would be! Let's cross it while we can. But how? The moat was at least 2–3 meters wide (6–9 feet) and at least one meter (3 feet) deep. We had no choice but to wade into the icy water. It was awful. Bandi carried his pregnant wife in his arms, while the rest of us crossed, climbing almost waist deep into the icy mess. Once on the other side, we frantically searched for the expected Austrian flag, but it was nowhere to be seen in the misty darkness of dawn. By now, we were totally lost. None of us had any sense of direction left, and we had no idea whether we were still in our poor enslaved Communist Hungary, or on the free soil of Austria. Then, someone remembered having a compass in his bag. After a lengthy search in the darkness he finally produced the precious little instrument. Huddling together, we tried to see what the little needle showed, but it was impossible to see anything in the darkness. Having found

The precious flame

a match, we created a tent with our heads, so that the outside world could not see its flickering little flame. Finally we got a reading. However, in spite of what the compass showed, the boys could not agree on the direction we were supposed to take. The girls did not join the argument. Wherever we looked in the semi-darkness, there were reeds, reeds, and more reeds, stubbornly sticking out of the frozen water. In the meantime, the disagreement over the direction got more and more pronounced, creating a few minutes of added tension within our group. Finally, we decided to proceed in what we thought was a north-westerly direction. We had hardly walked a hundred feet when the ground under us started to get softer and softer. It became obvious that we were lost in the midst of the swamps of Hanság. Yet, there was no way to return. As time went on, the high reeds all around us totally hid our bodies. We became desperate, yet had to press on. To make matters worse, the reeds stood in about 8 inches of icy water. Because of the November cold, the water was covered with a thin layer of ice. At every step, the ice splintered under our feet, submerging them into the icy water up to our shins.

Icy mess

As the reeds got thicker and thicker we had to stop again. "Do reeds get thicker towards the edge of a field or towards the middle?" became the puzzling question. Because none of us knew enough about the topic, it remained an unanswered question.

As expected, the longer we walked in the icy water, the worst our feet felt. Finally, after a few hours of such torture, Maria announced that she could not take another step. After a short discussion, two of the boys volunteered to carry her on their linked hands. By then, I was so cold and exhausted that I announced to the group that I wanted to stay there, lay down among the reeds and go to sleep. In no uncertain terms, Bandi forbade me to remain behind and gave me Maria's bag to carry instead. "Having none of your own," he commanded, "you might as well carry something and occupy yourself." Meanwhile the reeds were getting thicker and thicker and it was almost impossible to continue. We had to stop again and again. Finally, we decided that two of the boys should go in the front and break the reeds so that the ones who were carrying Maria, as well as the rest of us, could pass through. Now, the girls had to carry everyone's bags. I, who had no baggage of my own, became laden like a donkey with the luggage of others. We marched on for hours, but the reeds still did not have mercy on our exhausted, desperately struggling group.

Terrifying lights on the horizon

It was heart-breaking and most discouraging to see the never-ending sharp plants waving all around us in the early morning winter breeze. Meantime, our wet pants froze onto our bloody shins, cut to pieces from the cruel plants. The worst part was that we did not even have the security of knowing that we were on free soil. We did not know whether the end of the reed field meant Russian slavery, ÁVÓ torture, or freedom. Meanwhile, the sun finally started to peek out from the broken-up clouds of the cold November sky. Yet, we were still imprisoned in the merciless reed field. It looked more and more hopeless and our exhausted group was at the verge of total despair.

Miracle! We Made It!

Suddenly, we noticed a tiny pathway of cut-down reeds, in the midst of the thick reed field which was obviously the work of human hands. Never did a sign of humans mean so much to us as the tiny path! Even if we ran into Communist hands, we figured at this point, anything was better than freezing to death here amongst the reeds.

So we continued stumbling over the freshly cut stems into the unknown. Soon, the forest of reeds on both sides of the stubble path was getting thinner and thinner. Within a few hours, the merciless plants disappeared altogether.

A huge muddy field spread all around us. It was still covered with icy water. By then, our feet were so stiff from the cold that they had almost no feeling left. But at least the reeds were gone!

Far away on the horizon, we noticed a long embankment. As we approached it, we could see more and more clearly that, on the top of it, a well-maintained Austrian highway snaked along. The unexpected discovery filled us with hope and gave our exhausted frozen limbs new energy to carry on. We no longer felt the tormenting exhaustion of our bodies, the painfulness of our frozen feet, the wet coldness of our clothing, nor the tormenting hunger of our growling stomachs. Even the heavy bags we were carrying lost their weight. We were on free land!

A half hour later, nine happy persons stood on the Austrian highway in hot embrace, forgetting cold, rain, reeds, Russian guards, ÁVÓ officers, and search parties. Forgetting everything that had been bad, they stood in a long embrace on a free Austrian highway with tears in our eyes, looking back, saying farewell to our enslaved but deeply loved Hungarian Homeland.

Coat of Arms of Hungary

Epilogue

Great Reunion -- Half a Century Later

Although some of us "actors" have reunited or kept in touch during the ensuing decades in our respective adoptive countries, our refugee group has never been together as a whole. So, after 56 years, we decided to meet in Budapest. The date was set for September 13, 2012. Our goal was to walk through our escape route and find the Gombkötő family to thank them from the bottom of our hearts for so bravely hiding us in 1956 during our escape ordeal. But how could we find them after so many years? How could we find Hanságpuszta, that tiny little hamlet, near the Austrian border whose name has been changed since then?

Before leaving New York, I was determined to track down the whereabouts of the Gombkötő family. I went on the Internet and searched every possible topic without success. Then I wrote to the town halls of nearby villages, but nobody had information on the Gombkötős. With such dismal search results about the family's whereabouts, we decided to drive to the Hanságpuszta region and try our luck by knocking on doors in the small hamlet.

Then a small miracle happened. A few days before our planned meeting in Budapest, I went to my 55th high school class reunion. Although I never graduated because I escaped, I always return to the reunions. Today, the school has been restored to its pre-communist era glory, which we as youngsters never saw. It has been totally renovated, modernized and its original buildings returned to the nuns. It now spreads an entire city block. When we studied there during communism, it was an old dilapidated building. Two thirds of the school's property had been confiscated by the communists. They used this school as a propaganda tool to show the Western world that "yes, we allow private schools." All of us students were children of communist "social outcasts": aristocrats, educated people, rich merchants and well-to-do peasants. None of us were allowed to continue our studies in public schools beyond the mandatory grade school. We were destined to be manual laborers for life.

At any rate, the class reunion started with a Mass at the school chapel at 10 am, where an old priest mumbled through the service from which I understood absolutely nothing. But we sang and prayed and thanked God for still being on earth to enjoy our families, friends and each other.

From L to R: *Marika, Eszter, Anikó, György and wife Svetlana and Gábor (*second row).

After the Mass, we visited our old classroom and each of us said a few words – some of them not so few! -- about our families, activities, trials, tribulations, successes and hardships. Around 1 pm, we broke for a fantastic Hungarian lunch in the school cafeteria with Wiener Schnitzel, potatoes, salad, and a delicious cherry strudel to top it all off. The latter was so good that I even ate my neighbor's dessert. Luckily for me, she happened to be on a diet. After lunch, we continued our individual reports. Some of my classmates' stories were very emotional and they reaffirmed my conviction that if we examine people's lives, in addition to lots of happy moments, every family has its tragedies, sadness and pain as well. And those families that triumph over the tribulations of life and have unconditional love and faith are held together. Again, I felt very lucky for having had such warm, loving, parents and brothers, such a noble gentleman for a spouse and such loving and kind sons.

And now the miracle! After the individual reports, we were mingling amongst our class mates, having a great time. Just as I walked by Dr. Misi Balázs, husband of classmate Dr. Marika Pázmándy, both physicians, I could not help overhearing him mentioning "Hanságfalva," that tiny hamlet that we were planning to visit with my refugee friends. At first, I could not believe my ears. "Misi," I said, "did I hear you say Hanságfalva?" "Yes, you surely did," he replied. "But, it is such a small little place," I injected, "how do you know about it?" "How?" he looked at me with curiosity, "I have been the chief physician in that area for 35 years." "Oh, my God," I said, "then you might know some people there." "Of course I do," he replied. "I know many." "By chance, did you ever hear of the Gombkötő family? "I surely have," he said with a smile. "As a matter of fact, Marika Gombkötő (14 years old at the time) is a personal friend of ours. She is now the wife of Imre Szitás. She lives in a nearby town, Mosonmagyaróvár. Would you like her number?" I was elat-

Eszter, Gábor, Anikó, György

ed! As soon as I got home that night, I called Marika Gombkötő. She already knew about me, because Misi had spoken to her earlier. She and I were on the phone for at least an hour, just like old friends. Marika said she remembered me. She even remembered that her parents wanted me to stay with them and not expose myself to the danger of being shot to death by the Russian guards.

"Where there are seven" Erzsi néni told them, "there is room for an eighth!" What wonderful people they were! Sadly, by now both Erzsi néni and Jáncsi bácsi are in heaven.

I learned from Marika what I did not know, that Jancsi bácsi was a "csendőr" (gendarme). Csendőrség in Hungary was a much disciplined military type of police force assigned to keep order in villages. They were famous for their magnificent uniforms and handsome tall figures. The outfit was under the jurisdiction of the Ministry of the Interior. The members of this outfit were also persecuted by the communists and classified as enemies of the people.

I kept my lucky discovery of Marika's whereabouts a secret from my refugee friends until we met for breakfast in my Budapest apartment. Gábor flew in from Germany, Anikó from Austria, and I represented the United States. György and his wife Svetlana met us later at Marika's home. György bought a vineyard in north western Hungary and lives there with his wife. It was like old days. After some emotional hugs, we were engaged in such intense conversations that we did not leave the house until two hours after our planned departure.

When I told my friends about the miracle of finding Marika, Anikó remarked, "My dear Esther, this is definitely God's hand." I agreed with her. The discovery of the Gombkötős completely changed our original plans. Instead of going on a blind search to the Hanságfalva region, we were invited to Marika's home and she offered to accompany us and show us the house where her family lived in 1956. She also knew where the muddy country path was where we were walking for miles and miles during the rainy night of our escape before getting lost in the deep icy swamp of the Hanság.

When we arrived at Marika's home around 1 pm, the reception was touching. She was as sweet and loving as her parents had been. Her large home was as immaculate as the tiny little house where she and her six siblings grew up. György met us there and on the way to Hanságpuszta he invited all of us for lunch in a Hungarian csárda (country tavern) located by the banks of a small branch of the Danube river. It was a very romantic place that provided us another opportunity to chat and exchange 56 years' worth of news.

Then we took off with two cars to Hanságpuszta proper. It was raining cats and dogs just like the day of our plight 56 years ago. Although the small county roads where we were driving were no longer a muddy mess, at times they were still hardly passable. The huge potholes filled with water made driving a real challenge. Having driven over an hour in such conditions, we were all amazed. "Did we really walk this distance 56 years ago?"

Even by car it took us a long time just to reach the tiny Gombkötő homestead. The house no longer belongs to the Gombkötős. A middle aged couple lives there now. When they noticed us pulling into their muddy driveway, they immediately came out, invited us into their home and let us roam around the tiny place at will to reminiscence about the past. "Do you remember? The bed was here. Do you remember this is where the table stood?" We spent quite a bit of time at the house. Every one of us had some memories to share. "How could seven children fit into this tiny room?" we asked Marika in unison. "We managed," she replied, "There was a bed in every corner, sometimes in bunks." We were so excited that we almost forgot that the clock was ticking. At the end of our visit, our hostess offered us some homemade coffee cake and cookies. What warm hospitality it was!

Home of the Gombkötő family in the hamlet of Hanságpuszta, our hiding place — 56 years later.

It was amazing, however, how after 56 years, our recollections differed at times. We all felt, however, that the house was even smaller than we have remembered. *"My Escape, Memories of a Hungarian Teenage Freedom Fighter"* (this book) became our reference manual having been written within weeks after our escape. I can just imagine how many false facts are in history books because in olden days history was based on oral recollections.

After our memorable visit to the Gombkötő homestead, we took off towards the last stretch of our escape route. It was still raining, just like 56 years ago. This time, however, we had the luxury of automobiles, raincoats, boots and umbrellas. Moreover, it was not dark, there were no search lights and we did not have to lie in the mud to hide from the Russian guards. In spite of all the current "luxuries," the bumpy country road seemed much longer than our recollections told us. "How could we have possibly done this long distance on foot, in the mud, under those horrible circumstances?" asked Anikó at one point. György had a quick instantaneous response: "We were all young!"

Unfortunately, the constant rain made our current journey very difficult once more. The puddles on this tiny country road were so huge at times that the wheels of our cars totally submerged in them. We had to crawl to ensure that the bottoms of our vehicles didn't get scraped up. We stopped at several spots, got out of the cars, umbrellas, raincoats, boots and all, and reminisced about our escape. We took pictures by the *"Hanságfalva"* sign where nearby dogs came to greet us but this time with wagging tails. What a difference it was from the noisy barking that tormented us during our escape.

Even though driving was a challenge, the tiny country road now had plenty of gravel on its surface, unlike the muddy mess we had to cope with during our flight. As we were riding along the seemingly endless path, it was getting darker and darker and the road was getting more and more impassable by car. Finally, our hosts told us that due to the weather, it would be impossible to go all the way by car to the Hanság swamp. So we reluctantly decided to

Hanságtanya, Hanságfalva, Jancsimajor, Andau
(Indicated by the small circles on the map)

abandon our effort to see the swampy mess where long ago we challenged the rain, the ice, the search lights and the danger of being shot to death. We were a bit disappointed not being able to see the swamp, although we knew that none of us would have been able to identify the spot where we had entered it. In this, Marika and her son could not help us either because they were not with us during this phase of our escape.

So we turned around and returned to Marika's house to Mosonmagyaróvár. She offered us some delicious desserts she had baked in our honor. We read parts of *"My Escape,"* where I speak lovingly and with much admiration about her parents, Erzsi néni and János bácsi. In turn, Marika showed us photographs of her parents and her seven siblings who were young children at the time. "At our family get-togethers," she told us, "there are always about 35-40 people! We are a very close-knit family.

We love each other, help each other, and care for each other. That's what families are all about." Again, I felt very lucky that my family has the same values. Before we left her house, Marika gave Anikó and me a beautiful table cloth hand-stitched by Erzsi néni. "I know Mom wanted you to have these," she remarked. What wonderful hospitality! It was already dusk when we departed with the promise to return soon.

It was "Revolution" All Over Again -- an Eyewitness Account

In October of 2006, I flew to Budapest to commemorate and celebrate the 50th anniversary of the 1956 Hungarian Revolution, the powerful event that started the downfall of the Soviet Communist Empire. But, alas, because of the current political climate, the celebration turned into another revolution. On 17 September 2006, the current socialist Prime Minister Ferenc Gyurcsány (Hungarians call him a communist) was caught on tape admitting that his administrations lied about the dismal economic reality of Hungary, a lie that had gotten him re-elected the previous April. The radio aired the audio recording of his comments, *"We have obviously been lying for the last one and a half to two years."* (*"Nyilvánvalóan végig hazudtuk az utolsó másfél, két évet."*) Despite public outrage, the Prime Minister refused to resign, and a series of demonstrations started in Budapest. They soon swelled from 2,000 to about 8,000 demonstrators. I arrived in Budapest on October 19 to attend the planned commemorative events on October 23-rd. Instead, the very first evening I joined a demonstration organized by the opposition in front of the Parliament. It was a well-organized and well-disciplined gathering which started on time and ended on time. Subsequent demonstrations were similarly peaceful. The speakers reiterated the economic realities of the country and the dismal performance of the current government that had been wasting Hungary's resources for the past four-plus years. Although full of political sparks and patriotic poems, the demonstrations were even humorous at times when e-mails received by the opposition party were read to the public. These e-mails were often humorous political satires and so funny that the sea of people gathered on the square roared with laughter. By the time October 23rd arrived, the Gyurcsány government found it wise to barricade off the Parliament area where

Police in riot gear

Barricades were everywhere

the official celebration was to occur. It wanted to safeguard the dignitaries who arrived from all over the world, among them 54 heads of states or governments. That morning, when we arrived near the Parliament, huge police barricades blocked our way. They looked like tiger cages in a zoo. Behind them police officers were standing in full combat gear. I wanted to see the "official celebration" – the elegant Hussars riding into the square on horseback, the bands playing patriotic songs, the raising of the Hungarian flag, and more. But no one was allowed to cross the barricades. Many people started to gather where we were, some ex-patriots or "56 refugees" as we are called in the US, curious foreign tourists equipped with cameras, video recorders and other electronic equipment hoping to document the events for posterity. But all they could photograph was riot police behind the barricades.

The Parliament Wrapped in the Hungarian Flag

Abandoning the Parliament area, we decided to join the demonstration of the opposition, FIDESZ party. It started at 4 p.m. at the Astoria, a beautiful square in Budapest, the meeting point of four wide boulevards: Kossuth L., Rákoczi east/west and Museum Kőrút (circle), and Károly Kőrút north/south. When we got there, thousands blanketed the place stretching way into the side streets. A gigantic television screen projected the events. Patriotic poems were recited and speeches were delivered by party members, including a former Olympic athlete, a water polo player, whose team won the gold medal in 1956 against the Russian team. Finally, Victor Orbán, head of the Fidesz party and ex-Hungarian Prime Minister spoke. It was a dignified poetic speech that reiterated the wish of the Hungarian people: a truly free country, a country without lies, and a government whose members place country ahead of power-hungry egotism. Thousands of people spilled into the boulevards and watched the proceedings on a giant screen mounted high above the square. We stood in the middle of Károly Kőrút flanked by wall-to-wall people from every direction. The crowd was exhilarated, interrupting the speakers either with enthusiastic applause, whistle blowing or by harmonizing their emotions with *"Gyurcsán Get Out! Gyurcsán Get Out! Gyurcsán ("Gyurcsány takarodj, Gyurcsány takarodj, Gyurcsány takarodj!")* The gathering ended around 6 p.m. with the official blessings of religious leaders of three different denominations. The last one finished his prayer by adding "please be careful going home." This puzzled me. Why was he saying that?

After the final prayer, we slowly turned around with the crowd to head home on Károly Kőrút. The crowd was excited, happy and hopeful for a better future. Suddenly we heard shooting ahead. It must be fire crackers, we figured, and continued wherever the huge sea of humanity pushed us. A few minutes later, thick smoke rose above our heads from the direction of Deák Tér (square). Within seconds, we felt the painful effects of the teargas. People started to cough and wipe their streaming tears. Personally, it affected my lungs more than my eyes. Before we could grasp the reality of the situation, we heard yelling and screaming from ahead.

Suddenly about 25 feet ahead of us the heads of galloping police horses appeared. The galloping hoofs, like a sharp sword, cut straight into the panicked crowd. It reminded me of the parting of

Bird's eye view of the boulevard crossings

the sea by Moses. The crowd ahead of us was literally sliced straight in the middle by the galloping animals. We had only seconds to get out of their way. It was not an easy task because the crowd covered the total width of the wide boulevard. By then, the smoke was so thick that we could hardly see through our cascading tears. (The boulevard was closed to all traffic during the demonstrations.)

Meanwhile, the desperate crowd squeezed its way more and more toward the sidewalks which unfortunately were unable to accommodate the mass of people trying to find refuge there. To make matters worse, water cannons started to deluge us with gale force. They would have knocked all of us over had it not been for the thick crowd which held us upright from all sides. Within seconds, the horses came galloping across the middle of the now empty boulevard. By the way, horses don't appreciate teargas either. It seemed to drive them crazy. Try to show a horse how to scratch its stinging, burning eyes! Soon, rubber bullets started to fly between the teargas and the water cannons. They peppered the crowd like dried green beans spilled on the kitchen floor. Although the rubber balls don't penetrate the skin, nevertheless they cause huge bruises and, you can kiss your eyesight goodbye if your eyes get a direct hit.

Thick smoke shrouded the water cannons and the rubber bullets

Meanwhile, the sidewalk crowd started to panic. People were flowing like hot lava, pushing ahead with overpowering force. There was a giant man next to me whose head towered over the massive crowd. Just as I thought we were about to be crushed to death, the huge man calmly turned back toward the crowd, raised his long arm high above the crowd, and like a Greek god, calmly addressed the panicked crowd: "Please stay calm," he said, "We can all make it safe if you cool it. Let's not crush each other to death. Pull back" To my surprise, people listened, the pressure diminished somewhat and we could move again. Within ten minutes, the crowd reached one of the side streets and squeezed onto it becoming a paralyzed block of human flesh. We came to a screeching halt. Someone started to scream: *"ÁVÓ, ÁVÓ"* (the name of the Hungarian secret police during communist times). Within seconds, thousands of voices chimed in from people who blanketed the road. Then, the crowd chanted into its well-known slogan: *Gyurcsán get out! Gyurcsán get out! Gyurcsán get out! ("Gyurcsán takarodj!")*

I did not get home until midnight because police barricades blocked all the roadways, and no subways, street cars or buses ran midtown. As I stepped through the doorway of my Budapest apartment, my son was on the phone from New York. He watched the events in Budapest on CNN. "I just knew you were there," he said. "I am so glad you made it home safely." After I hung up the phone, I turned on the television. The reporter was talking about the number of injuries and showed the flashing lights of ambulances at the scene. I am lucky, indeed, I thought, to be home safely.

Actors in the Drama

Géza Ürmössy (Uncle Géza) was my father's friend, an agronomical engineer who worked near the Hungarian-Austrian border. He was the grandson of the famous Hungarian painter, *Gyula Benczúr*. Uncle Géza escorted his two sons, *György* and *Miklós*, his nephew *Gábor* and five others, including *Anikó* and myself to the Hungarian-Austrian border and helped us escape to freedom. Because of other family obligations, he remained in Hungary. After the Revolution was crushed, the communists retaliated. *Uncle Géza* lost his job as an engineer and he made his living by selling his hand-crafted decorative leather goods. During Gulyás Communism, he visited his sons in England several times. He died in Hungary and is buried there.

Esther Kandó Odescalchi, I am not only the teenage author of this document, but also one of the "actors" of the dramatic escape. All the other "actors" of this escape were my childhood friends.

During the revolution, when I heard on the radio that blood was desperately needed for the wounded freedom fighters, I immediately took off toward the hospital. In spite of the dangers, my parents whole-heartedly approved. For the first time in my life I became a blood donor and I still am. Nobody asked in those days how old you were. If you were healthy they gratefully accepted your blood.

After the escape, I went to the United States, got my Ph.D. in communications and for many years worked for IBM. I married the love of my life, Edmond, and we had two sons. Later, as a passion, I also earned my Dance Master's Certificate and became a professional ballroom dancer.

Anikó Csák Toro was my friend and classmate since first grade. Anikó also knew well the *Ürmössy* boys, because she spent many summers at their estate in northern Hungary.

During the revolution, *Anikó*'s parents, being very worried about their daughters' safety, did not allow Anikó and her sister to leave the house, so they could not actively participate in the revolution.

After our escape, *Anikó* went to a well-to-do aunt in Vienna who arranged for her to study at the Hungarian-language institute in Innsbruck. After graduation, she enrolled in the economic division of the university but after seven semesters she got married, left her studies and moved back to Vienna. She still lives there and for the past ten years works as a volunteer in a city hospital. During her active years she worked as a secretary and as German-Hungarian translator.

Miklós Ürmössy, the older son of Uncle Géza, was drafted into the Hungarian army two years prior to the Revolution. The communists did not allow him to continue his studies at the University because the communists considered his family "enemies of the people." He did not want to be a common working soldier, (as sons of families like his were destined to work in construction, road building, coal mines and the like.) Somehow, he succeeded entering the officers' school of the motorized unit of the army in Tata (a small town).

The day the revolution broke out, his entire unit was ordered to Budapest. No sooner did the soldiers arrive in the capital when their commander immediately joined the freedom fighters. From that moment on, they were transporting the wounded and the dead and/or delivered supplies to the freedom fighters non-stop. Then, when the Russian tanks inundated Budapest, he and many others had to flee. The returning communist government would surely have hanged him as a military deserter.

After our flight, Miklós went to England and worked for a construction firm that also financed his college education. He was with the company for 28 years and became one of its directors spending ten years in Saudi Arabia. Currently, he lives in California and runs his own digital imaging/printing business.

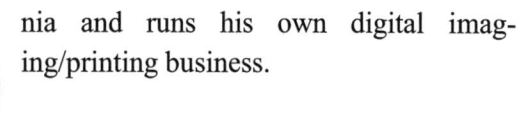

György Ürmössy is the younger son of *Uncle Géza*. During the revolution he drove a huge pick-up truck — without a license! — to supply weapons to the freedom fighters. He and Cousin Gábor would surely have been imprisoned had he not escaped.

After the escape, he and brother *Miklós* went to London and established their own successful business. Several years ago, *György* returned to Hungary, bought a vineyard near Lake Balaton and has enjoyed the country life ever since.

Gábor Benczúr-Ürmössy is a nephew of Uncle Géza and has been my friend since childhood. At the outbreak of the Revolution, he studied at an engineering facility of the University of Miskolc, a city located in northeast Hungary. As soon as news of the fighting in Budapest reached the city, the residents of Miskolc were ready for freedom.

During the revolution, *Gábor* and other students were manning the city's telephone and communications center as members of the newly formed National Guard (Nemzetőrség). The Center broadcast important news to the people day and night. After the escape, *Gábor* went to Germany where he still lives. He earned his Ph.D. in engineering and had a successful career at Volkswagen and Daimler-Benz. His memories of the 1956 Revolution are immortalized in the book: "Szemtanúk" ("Witnesses") (Marosvásárhely 2006).

Sára Maurer Ürmössy was already engaged to Miklós Ürmössy at the time of our escape. The couple got married in London and until the birth of her children, Sára worked as a bookkeeper. Because from 1965 on Miklós spent most of his time abroad, Sára was in charge of raising their children. In 1983 the couple separated and Sára still lives in London.

Bandi Soós (deceased) was already in his twenties and married at the time of our escape. Before the Revolution, Bandi earned his living creating designer leather watch bands. Because he took active part in the Revolution, he had to flee the country. After our escape Bandi went to England with his pregnant wife Mária and for a while worked in a decorative leather-wear company. Having learned the details of the English leather business, he soon founded

Bandi and Mária Soós

his own corporation. He produced such high-quality leather goods, that within a short period of time his company's reputation soared and it was listed on Queen Elizabeth's special *"By Appointment"* list. As a consequence, he received many orders from the Royal Palace and his business bloomed. After his untimely death, his daughter, Marianne took over the business but within two years, the company closed its doors.

Mária Maurer Soós (deceased) was already pregnant with her first child during our escape. Few months after arriving in London, she gave birth to a daughter, Marianne. A few years later, she had a severely handicapped son and spent her time taking care of him. Shortly after his death at age 19, Mária passed away as well.

The Silent Actors

Our beloved parents bore the consequences of our departure. They endured the returning communist government's retaliation for having had children who escaped to the West. Yet, throughout the years they remained silent participants of the Drama.

Without their love and support it would have been impossible for their children to make key decisions at such a young age and succeed as they all did in countries that were foreign to them.

From L to R: Uncle Gábor (Uncle Géza's brother), my Mother Mária, Aunt Rosette and my Father Ferenc. (Uncle Gábor and Aunt Rosette were Gábor's parents) (1957)

Anikó's parents Zoltán and Médy Csák

Historical Perspective

The Bridge at Andau

The Bridge at Andau is a small bridge over the Hanság canal, a small river that forms part of the border between Austria and Hungary. It is located near the village of Andau in Burgenland.

This is what remained of the bridge

During the Hungarian Revolution, the bridge was the escape route for more than 70,000 Hungarian refugees. After crossing the border, the fugitives walked the *"Road to Freedom,"* about nine kilometers, to the village of Andau. Refugee camps were set up in the village where the escapees were received with hospitality and kindness by the inhabitants of Andau and surrounding villages.

Trying to cross to freedom

On November 21, 1956, to prevent people from leaving Hungary, the Soviet troops blew up the bridge.

James Michener, in his famous nonfiction bestseller, chronicles the Hungarian Revolution of 1956. The author was at the Austro-Hungarian border during the period in which a significant wave of refugees fled Hungary. The book describes a historical event based upon interviews with eye-witnesses. The characters are based on real people but their names were changed for security reasons. The story examines the experience of different segments of Hungarian society, both before and during the uprising, such as students, workers, soldiers, secret police, and ordinary citizens. Michener takes the reader to the streets of Budapest, where unarmed young people, factory workers, and poorly equipped Hungarian soldiers fought the invading Soviet tanks.

"The Bridge at Andau is James A. Michener at his most gripping. His classic nonfiction account of a doomed uprising is as searing and unforgettable as any of his bestselling novels. For five brief, glorious days in the autumn of 1956, the Hungarian revolution gave its people a glimpse at a different kind of future—until, at four o'clock in the morning on a Sunday in November, the citizens of Budapest awoke to the shattering sound of Russian tanks ravaging their streets." (Book Review)

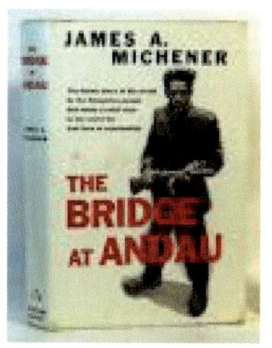

The book also tells the bittersweet story of the few days of freedom enjoyed by the citizens of Budapest before the Soviet tanks rolled in. In 1996, the 40th anniversary of the Hungarian Revolution, the bridge was rebuilt. Today, it is a symbol of cooperation and friendship between Austria and Hungary.

The Flag as a Symbol

Russian-style communist flag of Hungary

Flag from which the communist emblem has been cut out. It became the symbol of the Hungarian Revolution of 1956

The real Hungarian flag with the Hungarian coat-of-arms. The Revolution of 1956 paved the way toward the fall of the iron curtain and a free democratic Hungary.

The Hungarian National Anthem

Himnusz

The National Anthem of Hungary is a prayer to God, asking His blessing upon the people and the land of Hungary that have suffered so much during its turbulent history. The words were written by Ferenc Kölcsey, one of the great Hungarian poets, and the music was composed by Ferenc Erkel, who also wrote the national opera Bánk Bán, for a competition to decide the Anthem in 1823.

The Himnusz and its English translation (The first verse)

Ferenc Kölcsey
(1790-1838)

Isten, áldd meg a magyart
Jó kedvvel, bőséggel,
Nyújts feléje védő kart,
Ha küzd ellenséggel;
Bal sors akit régen tép,
Hozz rá víg esztendőt
Megbünhödte már e nép
A multat s jövendőt!

Ferenc Erkel
(1810-1893)

O, please God, bless the Magyar
With Thy plenty and good cheer!
Extend toward it Thy helping hand,
Where its foes to fight appear.
Whom faith has long been torturing;
Bring it happiness and joy;
This nation has already suffered
The sins of its past and future days.

The World Remembers the Heroes

The world still remembers those who have sacrificed their lives so that others can live in liberty. Many memorials have been erected all over the world honoring the 1956 freedom fighters.

1956 Memorial in Toronto

It was the 1956 Revolution that made possible the "*Gulyás Communism,*" the 1989 August 19th *Pan-European Picnic,* the collapse of Soviet dictatorship, the crumbling of the *Iron Curtain* and a free democratic Hungary.

The 1956 Monument in Boston Liberty Square

Memorial in Cleveland, OH, Commemorating the Hungarian freedom fighter with the Hungarian flag from which the freedom fighters cut out the communist emblem.

Communist Mementos Belong to the Past

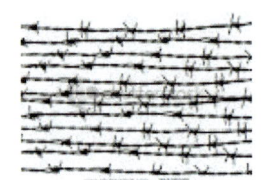

Barbed wire fences.

Stalin statues

The iron curtain

Guard towers ....where the order was to shoot!

Budapest is in Its Old Glory Again!

Collage by Nora Szabo

On August 20th Budapest celebrates St. Steven's day, the biggest national holiday

Hungarian Parliament in Budapest

The famous Váci Street is alive again

Fishermen's Bastion

A Glance at Hungarian History

During the Cold War, Soviet Russia terrorized the countries behind the iron curtain. Two events in Hungary hammered the first and last two nails into the coffin of Soviet Communism. The first was the *Hungarian Revolution of 1956* (even though it was defeated) and the second the *Pan-European Picnic* in 1989 when the nation dared to cut the iron curtain between Austria (the free Western World) and Hungary, allowing hundreds of East Germans to dash across to freedom.

Origins

The seven Hungarian tribes, led by Árpád, their leader, arrived to the Carpathian Basin in the 9th century. From 895 to 902 the whole area of the Carpathian Basin was conquered by them. Their outstanding horsemanship and military power allowed the Hungarians to conduct successful campaigns and raids as far west as Spain and as far east as the walls of Constantinople.

Saint Stephen, Hungary's first king was the son of Prince Géza and a descendant of Árpád. He converted the pagan tribes to Christianity and in December 1000 AD he was crowned with the Holy Crown of Hungary in the capital at the time, Esztergom. Hungary was recognized as a Catholic Apostolic Kingdom and the country remained a kingdom for one thousand years.

Mongol Invasion

During its long history Hungary was often the bumper zone between the East and West. In 1240 *Batu Khan* (1205-1255), the founder of the Mongol Golden Horde, defeated the Hungarian army and occupied the great Hungarian plains (1241 – 1242) leaving Hungary in ruins and half of its population wiped out.

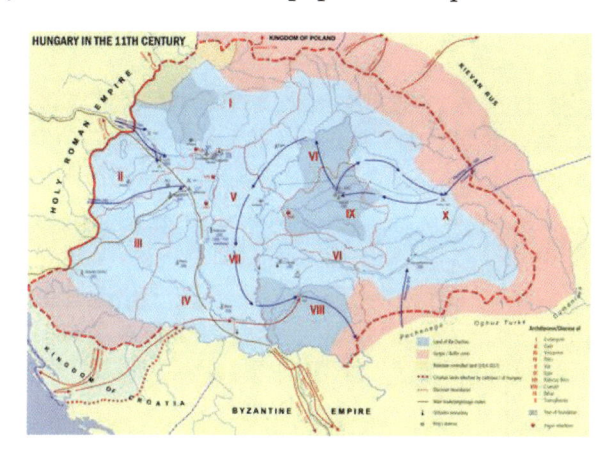

During the succession of able kings, however, Hungary gained huge territories and became one of the largest European kingdoms. By the fifteenth century, especially during the reign of *King Matthias* (1458-1490) it also became a Renaissance cultural center.

One Hundred Fifty Years of Turkish Occupation

In 1526 Hungary was again conquered. In their quest to rule the world, the Ottoman Muslim Turks, led by Suleiman the Magnificent (1520–1566), attacked the country and defeated the Hungarians. Thus began one hundred and fifty years of Turkish occupation. In 1541 Hungary was divided into three parts: the Turks ruled central and southern Hungary; the Habsburg dynasty governed west and north Hungary; and the Hungarians ruled the eastern part the country which after 1570 became the Principality of

Transylvania. It was not until 1686 that the Turks were finally expelled from Hungary.

The 1848-1849 Hungarian Revolution

During 1703-1711 the Prince of Transylvania fought against the Habsburgs, but his attempts failed. So did the *1848-1849 Hungarian Revolution* against them. It was not until 1867 that Hungary finally reached a compromise with the Habsburgs initiating the double-monarchy of Austro-Hungary. In 1873 Pest, Buda and Óbuda were unified forming Budapest. It became a major European city and cultural center.

World War I and the Treaty of Trianon

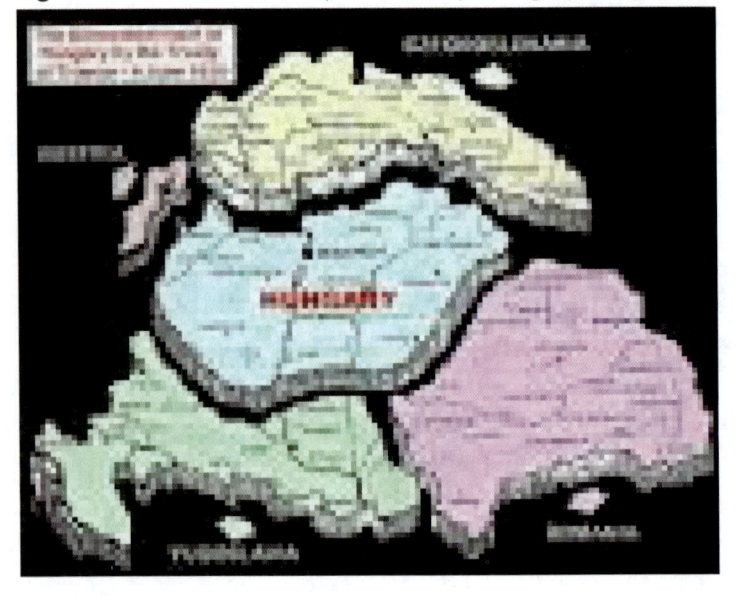

During the *First World War* (1914–1918) Hungary fought on the losing side and the monarchy collapsed. In the tragic *Treaty of Trianon* (1920), the peace agreement at the end of *World War I* between the Allies and Hungary, dismembered the thousand-year-old Hungarian Kingdom. The country lost 72% of its territory; its sea ports in Croatia; 8 of its 10 biggest cities; and 3,425,000 ethnic Hungarians found themselves separated from their motherland.

The principal beneficiaries of the territorial division of the pre-war Kingdom of Hungary were the enlarged Romania, and the artificially created countries of Czechoslovakia and Yugoslavia (the kingdom of Serbs, Croats and Slovenes). The territories assigned to these countries were mainly populated by ethnic Romanians, Slovaks and South Slavs. However, even today in some parts of Transylvania, Hungarians still form a large majority. For example, in Harghita, more than 84% are ethnic Hungarians (as of 2012).

In 1938, the *First Vienna Award*, mediated by the German and Italian Foreign ministers, returned to Hungary the region of "Felvidék" in southern Slovakia. In 1940, in the *Second Vienna Award* Hungary regained some two-thirds of the long-disputed Transylvania from Romania. However, in 1947, as a result of the Paris Peace Treaties, Hungary was obliged to return the territorial gains made in both agreements.

Between the Two World Wars

Miklós Horthy

In 1919, Hungary had a ninety day stint with communism under the cruel leadership of Béla Kún. Then, from 1920 to 1941, Hungary was a free democratic nation. The king was exiled and Miklós

Horthy (1920-1944) was the regent.

In 1933 Hitler became head of state, Supreme Commander of the Armed Forces and guiding spirit (Führer) of Germany's Third Reich. (The same year when FDR, became the 32nd President of the United States). In 1938 he annexed Austria. In 1939 he occupied Czechoslovakia and attacked Poland, starting World War II. To escape immediate occupation by the Germans, Hungary was forced to enter the war on Hitler's side. Count Teleki, the Prime Minister of Hungary, committed suicide in protest of Hungary's involvement on Hitler's side.

World War II and Yalta

In September 1939, *World War II* started and in 1944 the Nazis occupied Hungary. When Hungary tried to get out of the war, the Germans ousted Horthy and established their own puppet government headed by Ferenc Szálasy.

During the siege of Budapest, (December 24, 1944 to February 13, 1945,) Soviet troops surrounded the Germans who under direct orders from Hitler were not allowed to surrender. They all perished. During the 51 day siege, Budapest was destroyed and over half million or its residents lived without food, water, heat or electricity.

On June 6, 1944 the Allied forces landed in Normandy and eventually defeated Germany. On April 4th 1945 the Soviet Union "liberated" but then occupied Hungary.

In yet another tragic treaty, the *Yalta Conference*, (February 4–11, 1945), the United States, the United Kingdom, and the Soviet Union, represented by President Franklin D. Roosevelt, Prime Minister Winston Churchill, and General Secretary Joseph Stalin, respectively, Hungary's fate was sealed again. The country became a satellite of the Soviet Union and was imprisoned behind the iron curtain for forty years.

Prime Minister Winston Churchill, President Franklin D. Roosevelt, and General Secretary Joseph Stalin

In 1948 under Soviet communism, all Hungarian factories and businesses with over 100 employees were nationalized and in 1951 all "reactionary" elements of society (aristocrats, business owners, intellectuals, etc.) were deported to the countryside to live with peasant families and work in the fields.

The Hungarian Revolution of 1956

Although the *Hungarian Revolution of 1956* against communism and the Soviet Union was defeated, it was in reality the first step toward the fall of the I*ron Curtain*. The *1956 Revolution* was a spontaneous uprising against the communist regime. It lasted from October 23 to November 10, 1956. The entire nation was united in protesting the Soviet-imposed policies of the government.

The revolt began as a student demonstration but soon thousands of people joined the crowd as it marched through Budapest. A van with loudspeakers on the roof broadcast information to the people.

For a while there was hope

A student delegation compiled a list of demands, called the *16-point Student Demands,* and entered the radio building planning to broadcast its demands. However, the communist officials detained the delegation. When it became obvious that the students were detained, the crowd outside demanded their release. As a response, the State Security Police (ÁVÓ) fired upon the unarmed demonstrators.

The news spread like wildfire. Disorder and violence erupted throughout Budapest and spread quickly across Hungary. People from all walks of life organized into militias and were fighting the ÁVÓ and the Soviet troops. They released political prisoners and often executed or imprisoned pro-Soviet communists and

Students rally at front of the University

ÁVÓ members. The communist government fell and the newly formed government disbanded the ÁVÓ, declared its intention to withdraw from the Warsaw Pact and promised free elections.

By the end of October, the fighting had almost stopped. The nation hoped it had finally achieved liberty. Then suddenly, on the 4th of November, a huge Soviet force invaded Budapest and other parts of the country. Hungarian freedom fighters heroically resisted the invaders but by November 10, they had to succumb to the overpowering Soviet army. During the fight for freedom, over 2,500 Hungarians and 700 Soviet troops lost their lives. Over 200,000 Hungarians fled to the West as refugees. After the Soviets crushed the Revolution, the new Soviet-installed government retaliated by arresting, imprisoning or executing a great many innocent people. All public opposition was suppressed again.

The 16-point Student Demands:

1. We demand the immediate evacuation of all Soviet troops, in conformity with the provisions of the Peace Treaty.
2. We demand the election by secret ballot of all Party members from top to bottom, and of new officers for the lower, middle and upper echelons of the Hungarian Workers Party. These officers shall convene a Party Congress as early as possible in order to elect a Central Committee.
3. A new Government must be constituted under the direction of Imre Nagy: all criminal leaders of the Stalin-Rákosi era must be immediately dismissed.
4. We demand public enquiry into the criminal activities of Mihály Farkas and his accomplices. Mátyás Rákosi, who is the person most responsible for crimes of the recent past as well as for our country's ruin, must be returned to Hungary for trial before a people's tribunal.
5. We demand general elections by universal, secret ballot to be held throughout the country to elect a new National Assembly, with all political parties participating. We demand that the right of workers to strike be recognized.

6. We demand revision and re-adjustment of Hungarian-Soviet and Hungarian-Yugoslav relations in the fields of politics, economics and cultural affairs, on a basis of complete political and economic equality, and of non-interference in the internal affairs of one by the other.
7. We demand the complete reorganization of Hungary's economic life under the direction of specialists. The entire economic system, based on a system of planning, must be re-examined in the light of the conditions in Hungary and in the vital interest of the Hungarian people.
8. Our foreign trade agreements and the exact total of reparations that can never be paid must be made public. We demand to be precisely informed of the uranium deposits in our country, on their exploitation and on the concessions to the Russians in this area. We demand that Hungary have the right to sell her uranium freely at world market prices to obtain hard currency.
9. We demand complete revision of the norms operating in industry and an immediate and radical adjustment of salaries in accordance with the just requirements of workers and intellectuals. We demand a minimum living wage for workers.
10. We demand that the system of distribution be organized on a new basis and that agricultural products be utilized in a rational manner. We demand equality of treatment for individual farms.
11. We demand reviews by independent tribunals of all political and economic trials as well as the release and rehabilitation of the innocent. We demand the immediate repatriation of prisoners of war (World War II) and of civilian deportees to the Soviet Union, including prisoners sentenced outside Hungary.
12. We demand complete freedom of opinion and expression, freedom of the press and radio. We demand the creation of a daily newspaper for the MEFESZ Organization (Hungarian Federation of University and College Students' Associations).
13. We demand that the statue of Stalin, symbol of Stalinist tyranny and political oppression, be removed as quickly as possible and be replaced by a monument in memory of the martyred freedom fighters of 1848-49.
14. We demand the replacement of emblems foreign to the Hungarian people by the old Hungarian arms of Kossuth. We demand new uniforms for the Army which conforms to our national traditions. We demand that March 15th be declared a national holiday and that the October 6th be a day of national mourning on which schools will be closed.
15. The students of the Technological University of Budapest declare unanimously their solidarity with the workers and students of Warsaw and Poland in their movement towards national independence.

16. The students of the Technological University of Budapest will organize as rapidly as possible local branches of MEFESZ; decided to convene at Budapest, on Saturday October 27; organize a Youth Parliament at which the entire nation's youth shall be represented by its delegates.

The Pan European Picnic

The second and final event that helped tumble the Soviet Empire also happened in Hungary. It was the *Pan European Picnic,* a peace-demonstration held on August 19, 1989 by the Austrian-Hungarian border near the city of Sopron. It was organized by Otto von Habsburg, heir apparent of the former Habsburg dynasty, and Imre Pozsgay, (b. 1933-) a Hungarian ex-Communist politician who played a key role in Hungary's transition to democracy after 1988.

Otto von Habsburg

In a symbolic gesture, Hungary and Austria agreed to open a border gate for three hours between Sopronkőhida, Hungary, and Sankt Margarethen in Burgenland, Austria. Prior to August 19th, the organizers of the *Pan-European Picnic* had distributed pamphlets announcing the event. Before the *Picnic*, Hungarian border guards were ordered by the Ministry of the Inte-

Imre Pozsgay

Cutting the Iron curtain

rior not to bear arms that day and not to intervene in any way. As a consequence, on August 19th, more than 600 East Germans fled into Austria. The Hungarian border guards even helped the fugitives.

Angela Merkel

Subsequently, on the 11th of September 1989, Hungary opened its borders for East German and other Eastern European citizens. This was the first time that the border of an Eastern European country was opened for the citizens behind the Iron Curtain. Within a few months, more than 70,000 people fled to the West through Hungary. The Iron Curtain fell, and in 1990 the Soviet army left Hungary.

East Germans fleeing across the Hungarian Border

In 2009, the commemorative event of the 20th anniversary of the *Pan-European Picnic* was held in Sopronkőhida (I was invited). Many dignitaries attended the celebration. Angela Merkel, the Chancellor of Germany, thanked the Hungarians for their bravery and vision. *"Two enslaved nations broke the chains of slavery together .... And the Hungarians gave the wings to the East Germans for the hope of freedom."*

PanEuropean memorial in the Memorial Park near Sopron by Miklós Melocco was unveiled during the celebration

After the Iron Curtain Crumbled

In 1990 The Soviet army left Hungary and today, Hungary, with a population of 10,300,000, is a free democratic country. The Hungarian constitution guarantees human and civil rights just like the United States. The new constitution ensures the separation of powers among the judicial, executive, and legislative branches of government.

On March 12, 1999, Hungary became a member of the North Atlantic Treaty Organization or NATO (an intergovernmental military alliance created on April 4, 1949, whose member states agree to mutual defense in case of an attack by any external force). On May 1, 2004, Hungary was among the first former Communist countries that joined the European Union. The country moved from communism to liberal democracy and made a successful transition to the market economy. The Hungarian freedom fighters did not sacrifice their lives in vain.

Under the Blessed Silhouette of the Statue of Liberty

In the 1950s, Radio Free Europe (RFE) and the Voice of America encouraged resistance to Communist oppression. When the Soviet tanks rolled into Hungary during the *Hungarian Revolution* of 1956, the Hungarian nation was hoping that the western world would come to its aid, in particular, that the United States would intervene militarily. But no help came from anywhere and the revolution was brutally crushed.

Why did the United States Not Intervene?

Michael Logan, Correspondent of *The Christian Science Monitor* in an article entitled "Hungary's Lesson for Democracy Advocates" (October 23, 2006) enumerates the reasons for the United States not getting involved militarily during the Hungarian Revolution of 1956:

- *"The only way to have liberated Hungary in 1956 would have been military action. The US didn't want to start World War*

III." (Prof. Michael Fox, director of the Cold War Studies Center at the London School of Economics.)

- *"On November 1, 1956, a New York Times reporter told me if I were to dictate a declaration asking for help, he would print it. I told him I believed military intervention would end in nuclear war and Hungary would be the first to be evaporated."* (General Béla Király, commander of the newly formed 1956 *Hungarian National Guard* who desperately wanted his country to be free. Yet he realized that military intervention would lead to greater disaster.)
- *"The war in Iraq shows us, in retrospect, that the US was right not to intervene in the Hungarian upheaval of 1956. It would have unleashed a bloody and protracted war in Europe, even if it ended in victory."* (Olivier Roy, French Foreign Ministry consultant.)
- *"Sending United States troops alone into Hungary through hostile or neutral territory would have involved us in general war. . . ."* (Gen. Eisenhower in his memoir *In Review*)
- And then, there was another reason for western passivity. The Suez crisis blew up at the same time. *The UN was far too busy dealing with the fallout from Britain, France, and Israel's attempts to regain control of Egypt's waterway to worry about Hungary.* (Michael Logan, Correspondent of *The Christian Science Monitor,* "Hungary's Lesson for Democracy Advocates." October 23, 2006).

Thus, Hungary suffered alone, endured the retaliation of returning Soviet communists and lost many of its patriots who found refuge in the west.

Had it not been for the Western media's encouragement of the Hungarian freedom fighters to fight on, many Hungarians would feel differently about the military passiveness of the Western world during the Hungarian Revolution of 1956.

Although the United States did not get involved militarily to help Hungary, it welcomed the Hungarian refugees with open arms and gave them the opportunity to start a new life under the silhouette of Miss Liberty.

The author is grateful to her adopted country, for opening its shores to the 1956 Hungarian "freedom fighters." She enjoys this land of boundless opportunities where regardless of age, gender, national origin or religion, one can build a successful career -- with hard work, of course! -- and pursue any field of endeavor be it executive communication in industry, music, dancing, lecturing or building houses.

In these United States the sky is the limit

Dancing the Argentine Tango with Tom Nunes

At the piano during a recital at Kutshers Country Club performing Schubert's Arpeggione Sonata for flute and piano with Frank De Leeuw. November 19, 2005

Decorated with bull horns, lecturing on the PasoDoble

Playing the accordion for a dance group

On the stage with dance partner Ben Murtha performing the Viennese Waltz

111

In a Tango lift with Ben Murtha

Up on the rafters working on the electric wiring

Building the Pillar

This painting on slate has a special story. One evening a driver demolished our road-side pillar and I decided to re-build it. While I was working by the roadside, some people (mostly men) honked their horns as they drove by, some even stopped to talk to me and watch the pillar's progress. The pillar was soon completed and I did not give it another thought.

One day about a year later, a motorcycle pulled into our driveway and a strange man with a big beard appeared by the door. He was holding a big package under his arm. *Do you remember me?* he asked. *Not really*, I replied. *I am an artist,* he said, *and last year I stopped by to talk to you while you were working on your pillar. I have something for you,* he said, and pulled a large thin sheet of slate out of the package he held under his arm. *I painted this for you,* he said, *I hope you like it.*

My God, I responded with surprise, *this looks just like me. How could you paint such a life-like picture? Oh,* he responded with an mischievous smile, *before I drove off last year, I took your picture, that's how. I hope you like it.* Then, hardly giving me a chance to thank him, he turned around and drove off.

Oil painting on slate by K. Duchette (2012)

About the Author

Esther Kandó Odescalchi escaped from Hungary during the 1956 Hungarian Revolution that was crushed by Russian tanks.

She wrote these memoirs as a teenager in her native Hungarian immediately after her escape and translated them to English 50 years later.

She arrived to the United States as a refugee in 1957 and completed her education in the United States, earning a MS in library science and a Ph.D. in communications. After a career as a librarian, she joined IBM and worked in executive communications.

She is author of numerous technical and non-technical articles, three children's books and a play. She lectures and conducts workshops at colleges, universities, national and international organizations in the United States and abroad.

Odescalchi is also a professional ballroom dancer with a Dance Master's Certificate. She teaches, choreographs and performs.

The author is grateful to be in the land of opportunities, the United States, where hard work has its rewards. No other country provides the opportunities this land of liberty does. But, she also loves her native country, the now free democratic Hungary, for its culture, its unique language, its warm loving and patriotic people and, last but not least, for its "European touch."